Living in English

Basic Skills for the Adult Learner

Betsy J. Blosser

National Textbook Company
NTC a division of *NTC Publishing Group* • Lincolnwood, Illinois USA

Dedicated to the
Students and Staff of the
Illinois Migrant Council

Project Editor: Rebecca Rauff
Designer: Linda Snow Shum
Illustrator: Sandra D. Burton

Cover photos: Art Shay
            Karen E. Christoffersen

Acknowledgement is made to the following
for permission to reprint copyrighted material:
TOPS Business Forms, Inc., job application, 118-119.

1994 Printing

Contents

UNIT 5:
Purchasing Clothing

UNIT 6:
Dealing with Money

UNIT 7:
Purchasing and Maintaining an Automobile

UNIT 8:
Finding a Job

UNIT 9:
Identifying Community Services

UNIT 10:
Securing Health Services

APPENDIX
100 Want Ad Abbreviations

Getting Started

Activity 1: Greetings

A. Take turns reading the roles in these conversations. Notice the different ways you can greet a person, based on the situation and the person's age.

Ann:	Hi! How are you?
Roger:	Fine, thanks. How about you?
Ann:	Just fine, thanks.

John:	How've you been?
Sara:	Fine, John. How about yourself?
John:	O.K., Sara. No problems.

Stan:	Lucy, I want you to meet Alan. Alan, this is Lucy.
Lucy:	Hi, Alan! Pleased to meet you.
Alan:	Glad to meet you, too, Lucy.

Cindy:	Richard, this is my friend, Sally. Sally, this is Richard.
Richard:	Hi! It's good to meet you.

Phyllis:	Mrs. Bays, I'd like to introduce you to Robert Jones. Robert, I'd like you to meet Mrs. Bays.
Mrs. Bays:	Pleased to meet you.
Robert:	It's a pleasure.

B. Take turns reading these roles as the people leave the scene.

Linda: Glad to meet you.

Jim: Yes, it was nice meeting you. Hope to see you again sometime soon.

Linda: Yes. Goodbye.

Mike: It was good to see you.

Barbara: Yeah. Same here. Take care.

Mike: You, too. Goodbye!

Carol: It was good to talk to you.

Betty: Yes. See you soon.

Carol: O.K. Goodbye!

Betty: Bye!

C. Greet your classmates when you come to class next time, using the conversations in part A as a guide.

Activity 2: Names

Introduce yourself to the classmate sitting next to you. Then ask that classmate about other members of the class.

1. — My name is _____ . What's your name?

   — My name is _____ .

2. — What's his name?

   — His name is _____ .

3. — What's her name?

   — Her name is _____ .

Activity 3: People in the Classroom

Your teacher will point out people in class while saying the following sentences. Then you will repeat the sentences and answer the questions that follow.

1. She is a student.
2. He is a student.
3. You are a student.
4. I am a teacher.

Who is she?
She is a student. Her name is _____ .

Who is he?
He is a student. His name is _____ .

Who am I?
I am a teacher. My name is _____ .

Juan, who am I?
You are a teacher. Your name is _____ .

Activity 4: Things in the Classroom

Look around your classroom. Name the objects around you.

EXAMPLES:

It is a desk.
It's a chair.

Ask each other:

— What is it?

— It's a chalkboard.

Activity 5: Plurals

Point to items and people in the classroom while repeating the following sentences after your teacher.

It's a chair.
They are chairs.

He's a student.
They are students.

Activity 6: Numbers

1	one	6	six
2	two	7	seven
3	three	8	eight
4	four	9	nine
5	five	10	ten

Your teacher will show you a group of objects in the classroom. Count the objects and answer these questions.

— How many are there?

— Five pens.

— How many students are there?

— There are three students.

Activity 7: Adjectives of Color

The teacher will point to a real object and tell you the color of the object: red, yellow, blue, green, orange, purple, white, black, brown, gray, tan, pink. Then you will answer some questions about the object.

EXAMPLES:

(Pointing to a green chair)

— What is this?

— It's a green chair.

(Pointing to a blue pen)
— What color is this?

— It's blue.

(Pointing to a yellow pencil)

— What color is the pencil?

— The pencil is yellow.

(Pointing to a red pen)

— Is this a blue pen?

— No, it isn't. It's red.

Activity 8: Family

A. Study and discuss the relationships among the family members shown below.

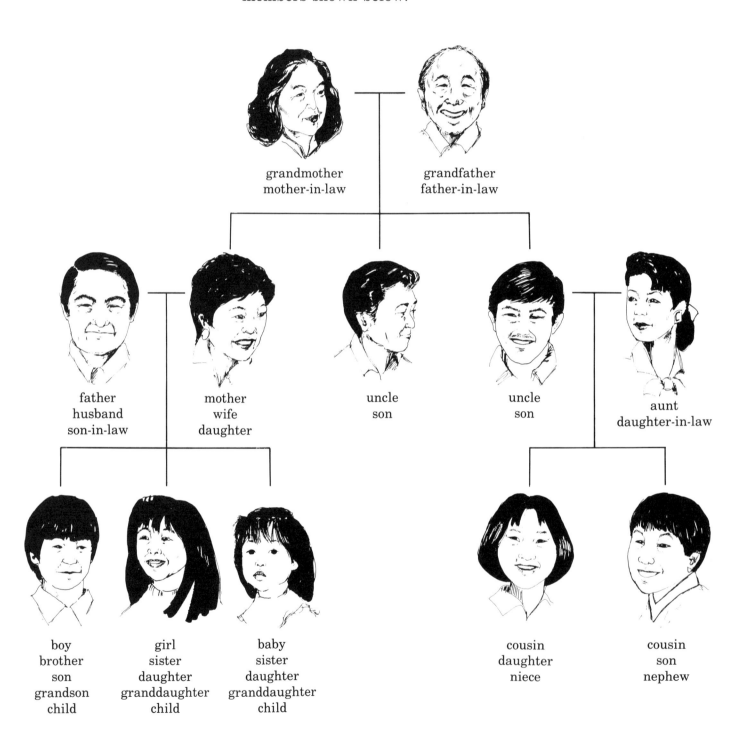

B. Looking at the chart, ask and answer the following questions. Use the names of family members to fill in the blanks.

— Who is she?

— She is a ___(mother)___ .

— Who is he?

— He is a (grandfather).

Then refer to each other. Ask and answer the following questions, using family names to fill in the blanks.

— Are you a ___(brother)___ ?

— Yes, I am.

— Are you a ___(daughter)___ ?

— No, I'm not.

C. Bring in photos of your family. Your teacher will ask you questions about them. Answer the questions.

EXAMPLES:

— Who is she?

— She is my sister.

— Who is he?

— He is my uncle.

— Who are they?

— They are my grandparents.

Activity 9: Negatives

Look at the objects your teacher points to. Listen and repeat the statements.

EXAMPLES:

It isn't green.
It's blue.

He isn't a student.
He's a teacher.

There aren't two chairs.
There's one chair.

They aren't my brothers.
They're my uncles.

Activity 10: Short Answers

Look at the pictures and objects your teacher points to. Answer the questions you hear.

EXAMPLES:

— Is it a table?

— Yes, it is.

— Is she your grandmother?

— No, she isn't.

Activity 11: Days of the Week

Look at a calendar and answer your teacher's questions.

EXAMPLES:

— What day is it?   — What day is today?   — What day is tomorrow?

— It is Wednesday.   — Today is Monday.   — It's Saturday.

UNIT 1

Making Wise Purchases in a Grocery Store

LESSON 1

Meal Planning

Activity 1 Go into your classroom "kitchen" with a classmate. Look to see what items are there, and make a shopping list of items that are <u>not</u> in the kitchen. Your conversation will sound like this:

— Let's make a shopping list.
— What do we need?
— We have eggs. We need bread.

— Do we need vegetables?
— Yes. We have celery. But we need lettuce.

— What else do we need?
— We have meat. We need beans and rice.

— What about milk?
— We need milk. We have cream.

Activity 2 Go into the kitchen in pairs. Take turns asking and answering questions about what you have and what you need.

EXAMPLES:

— Do we have eggs?
— Yes, we have eggs.

— Do we need vegetables?
— Yes, we need tomatoes, corn and peas.

— Do we need bread?
— Yes, we need bread.

— Do we need meat?
— Yes, we need meat.

Activity 3

A. Practice the names of the grocery items in the pictures.

B. In pairs, practice asking and answering the following questions.

— Do you need ___(1)___ ?

— Yes, I need ___(1)___ .

— Does she need ___(3)___ ?

— Yes, she needs ___(3)___ .

— Do they need ___(5)___ ?

— Yes, they need ___(5)___ .

— Do you need ___(7)___ and ___(8)___ ?

— Yes, I need ___(7)___ and ___(8)___ .

— Do we want ___(11)___ ?

— Yes, we want ___(11)___ .

— Does Sara want ___(13)___ ?

— Yes, Sara wants ___(13)___ .

— Does Juan want ___(15)___ ?

— Yes, Juan wants ___(15)___ .

— Do you have ___(2)___ ?

— Yes, I have ___(2)___ .

— Does he have ___(4)___ ?

— Yes, he has ___(4)___ .

— Do you have ___(6)___ ?

— Yes, we have ___(6)___ .

— Does she have ___(9)___ and ___(10)___ ?

— Yes, she has ___(9)___ and ___(10)___ .

— Do the children want ___(12)___ ?

— Yes, they want ___(12)___ .

— Do you want ___(14)___ ?

— Yes, I want ___(14)___ .

— Do you want ___(16)___ ?

— Yes, we want ___(16)___ .

C. Use other grocery items to practice the questions.

D. Make a shopping list from the items that someone either wants or needs.

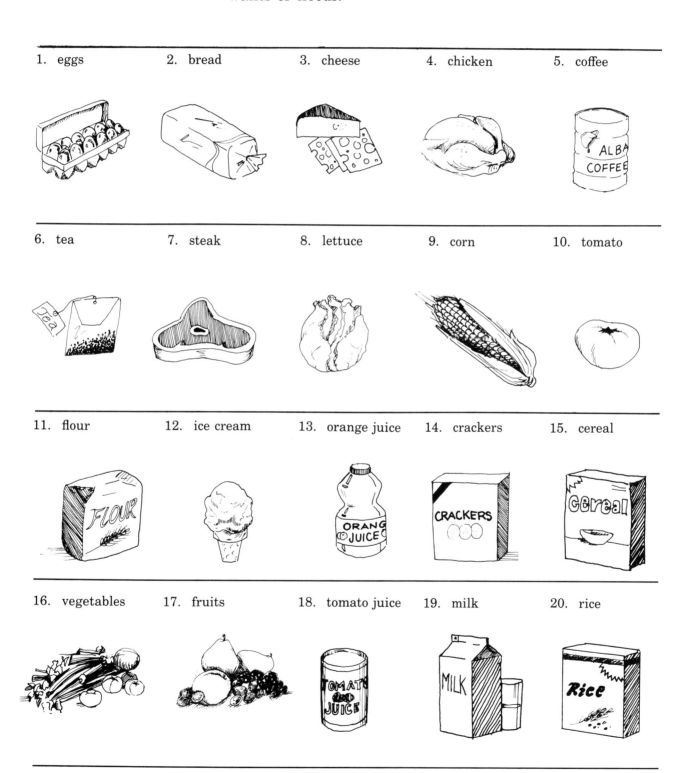

1. eggs

2. bread

3. cheese

4. chicken

5. coffee

6. tea

7. steak

8. lettuce

9. corn

10. tomato

11. flour

12. ice cream

13. orange juice

14. crackers

15. cereal

16. vegetables

17. fruits

18. tomato juice

19. milk

20. rice

Activity 4

Practice these conversations in pairs, using the materials your teacher provides.

8:00 A.M.

— Are you hungry?

— Yes, I am.

— Do you want breakfast?

— Yes, I want breakfast. I want eggs, bacon, toast, juice, and coffee.

12:00 P.M.

— Is she hungry?

— Yes, she is.

— Does she want lunch?

— Yes, she wants lunch. She wants soup, a sandwich, milk, and an apple.

6:00 P.M.

— Are they hungry?

— Yes, they are.

— Do they want dinner?

— Yes, they want dinner. They want chicken, rice, squash, a salad, and ice cream.

9:00 P.M.

— Is he hungry?

— Yes, he is.

— Does he want a snack?

— Yes, he wants a snack. He wants cheese and crackers.

Activity 5

Practice the conversations below.

— I have cereal, milk, bacon, and orange juice for breakfast.

— It's a good breakfast.

— We have fish, potatoes, green beans, bread, and peaches for dinner.

— It's a good dinner.

— She has cottage cheese, carrots, and fruit for lunch.

— It's a healthy lunch.

— They have celery and peanut butter for a snack.

— It's a healthy snack.

Activity 6

A. Take turns reading the following passage.

FOODS FOR HEALTH

People need healthy food. We need foods from the four food groups. They are meats, dairy foods, grains, and fruits and vegetables. We eat meat, eggs, cheese, and beans for protein. We eat cereal, potatoes, and bread for carbohydrates. We eat milk, yogurt, and cottage cheese for calcium. We need vitamins, too. Oranges, grapefruit, and lemons are citrus fruits. They have vitamin C. Carrots and liver have vitamin A. Nuts, grains, and yeast have vitamin B.

Meats

Dairy Foods

Grains

Fruits and Vegetables

B. Answer the following questions.

1. What foods have protein?
2. What are citrus fruits?
3. What foods have vitamin A?
4. What are the four food groups?

Purchasing Food

Activity 1

A. In pairs, ask and answer the questions below. Look at the shopping list to find the answers.

B. Take the roles of a grocer and a shopper, two shoppers, or a parent and a child to practice the questions and answers.

Do you need bread?
Yes, I need a loaf of __bread__ .

Do you need milk?
Yes, I need a carton of _____ .

Do you want lettuce?
Yes, I want a head of _____ .

Do you want peanut butter?
Yes, I want a jar of _____ .

Do you need meat?
Yes, I need a pound of _____ .

Do you need eggs?
Yes, I need a dozen _____ .

Do you want salad dressing?
Yes, I want a bottle of _____ .

Do you want soup?
Yes, I want five cans of _____ .

Shopping List
bread
meat
milk
eggs
lettuce
salad dressing
peanut butter
soup

Activity 2

Go into the classroom grocery store in pairs and take a shopping list (from Lesson 1, Activity 3D) with you. Use the shopping list to decide what you need or want at the store. Ask and answer questions like these:

Do you need vegetables?
Yes, I do.

Do you want lettuce?
No, I don't. I want carrots and squash.

Do you want tomatoes?
No, I don't. I want onions.

Do you need soup?
Yes, I do.

Do you want tomato soup?
No, I don't. I want mushroom soup.

Do you need meat?
Yes, I do.

Do you need baked goods?
Yes, I do.

Do you want a cake?
No, I don't. I want cookies.

Do you need fruit?
Yes, I do.

Do you need oranges?
No, I don't. I need apples.

Do you want pears?
No, I don't. I want peaches.

Do you need dairy products?
Yes, I do.

Do you want a quart of milk?
No, I don't. I want a half gallon of milk.

Do you need a half gallon of ice cream?
No, I don't. I need a pint of ice cream.

Do you want cottage cheese?
Yes, I do. I want a carton of cottage cheese.

Do you want beef?
No, I don't. I want pork.

Activity 3

In pairs, take the roles of a grocer and a shopper. Use grocery materials as you ask and answer the following questions.

Do you have skim milk?

No, we don't. We have whole milk.

Do you have brown rice?

No, we don't. We have white rice.

Do you have fresh fish?

No, we don't. We have frozen fish.

Do you have corn tortillas?

No, we don't. We have flour tortillas.

Do you have fresh tomatoes?

No, we don't. We have canned tomatoes.

Do you have salad oil?

Yes, we do. We have two brands of salad oil.

Do you have potatoes?

Yes, we do. We have two kinds of potatoes.

Do you have a sale?

Yes, we do. We have a sale on orange juice.

Activity 4

A. Ask and answer these questions using ads from your local newspaper.

How much is the lettuce?

It's _____ cents a head.

How much is the salt?

It's _____ cents a box.

How much are the eggs?

They're _____ cents a dozen.

How much are the pickles?

They're _____ a jar.

How much are the grapes?

They're _____ cents a pound.

How much is the cheese?

It's _____ a pound.

How much is the milk?

It's _____ a gallon.

How much are the cookies?

They're _____ a package.

How much are the potato chips?

They're _____ a bag.

B. Add the name of a store to the questions (e.g., "How much are the eggs at Kroger's?"). Compare the prices of the same product at different stores.

Activity 5

Put prices on the foods in your classroom grocery store. Take the roles of two shoppers or of a grocer and a shopper in practicing the conversations that follow.

Customer: How much are the apples?

Grocer: They're forty-nine cents a pound.

Customer: They're a good buy. I want three pounds of apples.

Customer: How much is the ground round?

Butcher: It's a dollar ninety-five a pound.

Customer: It's expensive. I want ground chuck.

Customer: How much are the peaches?

Grocer: They're eighty-nine cents a pound.

Customer: They're high. I want oranges.

Customer: How much are the cookies?

Grocer: They're on sale. They're ninety cents a package.

Customer: They're a good buy. I want a package of cookies.

Customer: How much is the turkey?

Butcher: It's ninety cents a pound.

Customer: It's expensive. How much is the chicken?

Butcher: It's seventy cents a pound.

Customer: I want chicken. I don't want turkey.

Customer: How much is the ice cream?

Grocer: It's ninety cents a quart.

Customer: It's expensive. How much is the sherbet?

Grocer: It's seventy-nine cents a quart.

Customer: I don't want ice cream. I want sherbet.

Customer: How much are the tomatoes?

Grocer: They're fifty-seven cents.

Customer: How much is the tomato sauce?

Grocer: It's on sale. It's thirty cents a can.

Customer: Good. I want six cans of tomato sauce.

Activity 6

A. Set up a check-out counter in your classroom grocery store. Using play money, take the roles of the grocer and customer, and practice this conversation.

Customer: How much are the groceries?

Grocer: They're thirty-three twenty. Do you have coupons?

Customer: Yes, I do.

Grocer: Do you have food stamps?

Customer: No, I don't.

Grocer: The bags are heavy. Do you need help?

Customer: Yes, I do. Thank you.

B. As the grocer, ring up the grocery items that the customer wants to buy on an adding machine or a hand calculator. Complete the purchase.

C. As the customer, use food stamps to buy your groceries.

D. As the customer, take coupons to the store and use them to buy your groceries. The grocer (as in C) should deduct the amount of the coupons from your bill.

UNIT 2

Arranging Housing for the Family

LESSON 3

Finding Housing

Activity 1

Practice these conversations between realtors and people looking for housing.

Husband: We want to rent a house.

Realtor: Do you have children?

Wife: Yes, we do. We have four children.

Realtor: How much space do you need?

Husband: We need three bedrooms.

Realtor: I have a house for you. It's near a school. Do you want to see it?

Wife: Yes, we do.

Realtor: I have an apartment for you. It's in a nice building and the rooms are big.

Jerry: Where is it?

Realtor: It's on Grant Street.

Jerry: What is the rent?

Realtor: It's three fifty a month.

Jerry: Good! I want to see it.

Activity 2

A. Richard Chen, Mr. and Mrs. Navarro, the Stones, Rachel Betz, and the Lee family are all looking for housing. They each call a realtor. Role-play their conversations.

Mr. Chen:	I want to rent an apartment.
Realtor:	What do you need?
Mr. Chen:	I need two bedrooms and one bathroom.
Realtor:	How much do you want to pay?
Mr. Chen:	Three hundred dollars a month.

Mr. & Mrs. Navarro:	We want to rent a house.
Realtor:	What do you want?
Mr. & Mrs. Navarro:	We want a three-bedroom house with two bathrooms.
Realtor:	How much rent do you want to pay?
Mr. & Mrs. Navarro:	Five hundred fifty dollars a month.

Stones:	We need housing.
Realtor:	Do you want an apartment?
Stones:	No, we don't. We want a house.
Realtor:	Do you want to rent?
Stones:	No, we don't. We want to buy.

Ms. Betz:	I need to find an apartment.
Realtor:	What do you want?
Ms. Betz:	I want a studio apartment near the subway.
Realtor:	What do you want to pay?
Ms. Betz:	Two hundred seventy-five dollars a month.

Lees: We want to find a house.

Realtor: How much space do you need?

Lees: We need three bedrooms and a backyard.

Realtor: Do you have children?

Lees: Yes, we do. We have three children. We also have pets.

B. Answer the following questions.

1. What does Richard Chen want?
2. How much does he want to pay?
3. How many bedrooms do the Navarros want?
4. Do they want to buy a house?
5. Do the Stones need housing?
6. Do they want to rent an apartment?
7. What does Rachel Betz want?
8. What does she want to pay?
9. Do the Lees need four bedrooms?
10. Do they have children and pets?

Activity 3

Draw a line from each question to an appropriate answer, as shown.

Where is the apartment?	It's in the garage.
Where is the bathroom?	It's next to the bedroom.
Where is the laundry room?	It's in the attic.
Where is the house?	It's in a quiet neighborhood.
Where is the furnace?	It's on the second floor.
Where is the storage space?	It's in the basement.

Activity 4

A. Name the various rooms in a typical house.

B. Take different roles to practice the conversations.

— I need to find an apartment.
— What's in the newspaper?
— There are two apartments. One is expensive. The other one is reasonable.
— How much is the rent?
— It's three forty a month including utilities.

— We want to rent a house.
— What's in the want ads?
— There's a two-bedroom house with a fireplace and a yard.
— Where is it?
— It's in a quiet neighborhood near public transportation.

— We want to find a house.
— What's in the newspaper?
— There are three houses for rent and two houses for sale.
— Do you want to rent?
— No, we don't. We want to buy.

— I need to rent an apartment.
— What's in the want ad section?
— There's an interesting apartment. It has one bedroom, a swimming pool, and air conditioning.
— Is it furnished?
— No, it's not. It's unfurnished.

— We want to buy a house.
— What's in the newspaper?
— There's a nice house. It has three bedrooms and two baths. There's a basement and an eat-in kitchen.

Activity 5

A. Read the want ads below, making sure you understand all the abbreviations used in the ads. A list of want-ad abbreviations and their meanings is provided in the appendix.

B. Using the want-ad section shown here, look for ads to match the houses and apartments described in Activity 4.

Rent-Apts. N.

MEADOWLAKE HOSP.
AREA
4629 N. WINCHESTER
Get it while it's still a bargain. First-class, second-hand beautiful courtyard bldg on tree-lined street. Near Meadowlake Hospital. Heat, hot water & applcs inc. Resident engineer.
1 Bedrm Apts $375
For appt., 555-8171 wkdays til 5 pm. Other times 555-6290

622 W. Wellington, 3½ rms, 1BR, 3rd flr. Wood burn. frplc, w/w carpt. Mod kit/bath. Sundeck. No pets. Sublet March 1 to April 30, opt to renew. $625/mo. Call 555-9736

LINCOLN PARK: Sublet lg bi-level studio, track lighting, hrdwd fls, dshwshr, reserved prkg avail. $412/mo. March 1st occ. 555-4231 lve msg

1423 FARWELL: Nr Lk, park & L. Lg sunny 5 rm. $550. Hdwd flrs dec. 555-1976 or 555-0016

E. ROGERS PK. &
GLENLAKE
Avl immed. Extra lrg 1BRs & 2BRS, LR/DR, kit w/new cab, newly sanded hdwd flrs, Sec. 8 OK. GD REFS REQD. 555-2708

2828 N Cambridge (560W) Studio $370, 1BR $470. 2BR also avail. Nr Linc Pk & shpg. Gas/ht incl Engineer 555-9789 CHARLES REALTY 555-8600

Rent-Apts. Furn. N. W.

KEDZIE & IRVING PK-Studio, lrg main rm, walk-in closet, crptd, util inc. 555-8691

MONTROSE-PULASKI, 2½ rm studio, $340. W/W cptg, incl. heat. Quiet bldg. 555-9058

BELMONT/CICERO
Pleasant 2 rooms. $360/mo+ security, utils incl. 555-1935

Houses For Sale

R. E. Houses S.

$42,500 2BR RANCH
128TH/HALSTED
2 Garage. Let's talk. FHA/VA
JONES REALTY 555-7200

Georgian brick, 4 BR, 1½ baths, 2 rm attic, 4 rm bsmt
Waverly Home Sales
Call 555-7413

R. E. Houses S. W.

4BR house, Beverly Hills area, newly rehabbed. Contact Mr. Conrad 555-2268

Owner. 3 BR brk ranch (8300S-4600W), fam rm, refinished in/out. ($70's) 555-2779.

R. E. Houses N.

NORTH CENTER ST.
3 BDRM $73,900
JONES REALTY 555-7200

WEST ROGERS PK. 1ST OFFER Jumbo Georgian! 7 Rms, 3 BR, Multi BA, Main Fl. Den, Lg. Eat In Kit. w/Newer Appliances, Fin Rec Rm, 2½ C Gar. 130's.
WRIGHT 601 555-4200

EDGEWATER $39,900
3 BEDROOM T/HOME
Full bst. 1½ baths. Gas heat. 1 Block to lake, trans, shops. Off street prkg. FHA or VA O.K.
BURNS/LEE
(T273) 555-4900

$Value You Haven't Seen
5200N-5200W. Sparkling 2 BR brk ranch, hdwd flrs, nat wdwrk, newer furn & roof. Tastefully decor. Mid $90's

6800W-3500N. Lrg house-lrg LD/DR-3 lrg bdrms, lrg pnld bsmt, lrg double lot. In $90's
COLE/FLINT REALTORS
5860 W. HIGGINS
555-2012

Nice bungalow 8 rms, 4 BR, 2 bas, attic has 4 rms. Anxious
Waverly Home Sales
Call 555-7413

Belmont & Austin brk cln 6rms 3BR, 2c-gar. $92,000. Make offer. Tri-Lakes Rlty 555-9640

NORTH AUSTIN
Reduced $8,000 to $49,900!! 2 bdrm + htd porch, brk bung. Well maintained, 2 car garage with opener. Hurry! Call now! Rossner Realty 555-5601

★★EDISON PARK
Great location for this 3 bdrm beauty + brick addition, den on 1st floor. Priced right Tyler-Moore 555-8300

LOGAN SQ VICTORIAN!
1st offer. 1890's vintage 2 story, all 3 bdrms up! It's a real charmer w/open stairs, natural wood, 1½ modern baths & oversize cab kitch. In $70's. KATE McGAW RLTY 555-8500

★★MOVE RIGHT IN
This custom brick w/new kitchen, built in range, new electric, new garage. Call now Tyler-Moore 555-8300

Activity 6

A. Practice the roles of the people in each conversation below.

Realtor: This is the house.

Man: It's a large house with a nice yard.

Woman: Where is the school?

Realtor: It's on Madison Street.

Woman: Are there children in the neighborhood?

Realtor: Yes, there are. This is a family neighborhood.

Man: Good. We like the house.

Realtor: This is the apartment.

Client: I like it. The rooms are large and it's in a convenient location.

Client: How much is the rent?

Realtor: It's three oh five a month.

Client: Good. I want to rent it.

B. Practice the first conversation with each of the following changes:

1. The house has a fireplace and a two-car garage.

2. There are no children in the neighborhood.

3. The couple doesn't like the house.

C. Practice the second conversation with each of the following changes:

1. A couple wants to rent the apartment.

2. A woman doesn't like the apartment.

3. The apartment has two bedrooms and a view of the city.

LESSON 4

Getting Settled

Activity 1

A. Practice the conversation, taking the roles of an apartment manager and a prospective tenant.

Apartment manager: This is a one-year lease. The rent is due on the first of the month.

Prospective tenant: Do I pay the landlord?

Apartment manager: Yes, you do.

Prospective tenant: Is there a security deposit?

Apartment manager: Yes, there is. It's two hundred dollars.

Prospective tenant: What are the utilities?

Apartment manager: They're gas, electricity, water, and garbage pick-up. The tenant pays the utility company and the city.

Prospective tenant: O.K. Where do I sign?

Apartment manager: On this line.

B. Answer the following questions.

1. Do you live in an apartment?
2. Do you have a one-year lease?
3. Do you pay rent?

4. When is the rent due?
5. Who is your landlord?
6. What are your utilities?

Activity 2

A. Practice the conversations.

Resident: Are you new in the building?

Newcomer: Yes, we are. We're moving into apartment six.

Resident: Good! I live in number nine. Welcome!

Newcomer: Thanks! It's good to meet you.

Neighbor: Are you new in the neighborhood?

Newcomer: Yes, we are. We're moving into the house next door.

Neighbor: Good! Welcome to the neighborhood. Do you have children?

Newcomer: Yes, we do. Karen is seven and Steve is nine.

Neighbor: Our children are about the same ages. This is a good neighborhood for children.

B. Substitute the following for "moving into" in each of the conversations.

1. renting
2. living in
3. buying
4. subletting

Activity 3

A. Practice these conversations, taking the roles of a mother and child talking.

Child: The movers are here.

Mother: Good. Where is your father?

Child: He's parking the car.

Mother: Where are the movers?

Child: They're parking the truck.

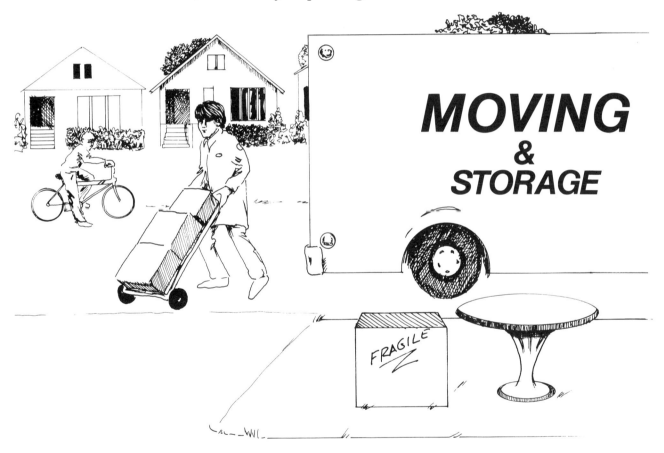

B. Practice the conversations again, substituting the appropriate form of these words for "parking."

1. move   5. lock

2. drive   6. open

3. back up   7. load

4. unload   8. pack

Activity 4

A. Practice these questions and answers, taking the role of a mover and a client. Use the names of the pieces of furniture shown in the pictures.

Where do you want the ___1___ and ___2___ ?
In the living room.

Where do you want the ___3___ and ___4___ ?
In the bedroom.

Where do you want the ___5___ ?
In the dining room.

Where do you want the ___6___ ?
In the hall closet.

Where do you want the ___7___ and ___8___ ?
In the kitchen.

Where do you want the ___9___ ?
In the bedroom closet.

B. Practice the same questions with different pieces of furniture and household items.

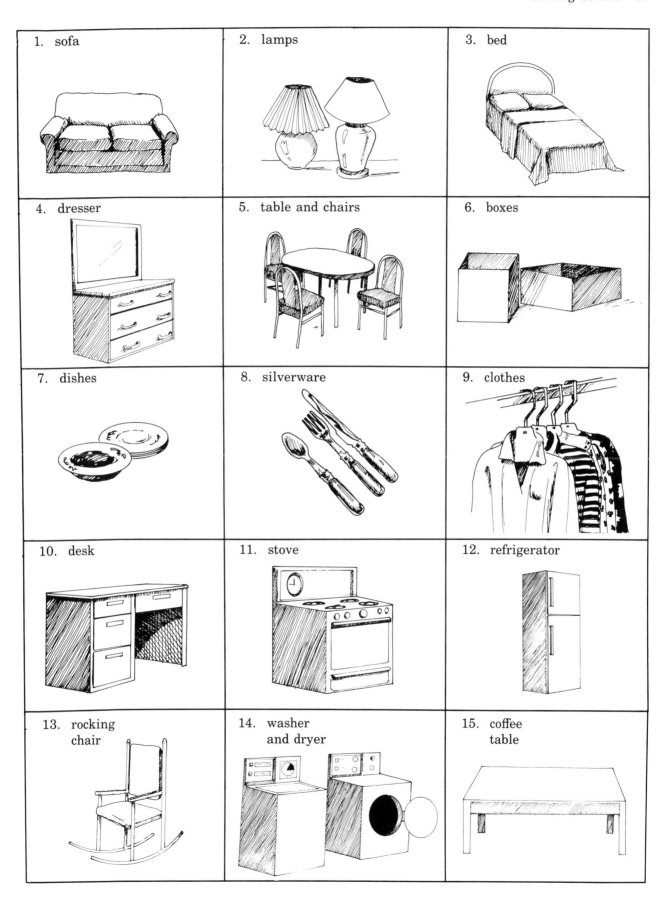

1. sofa
2. lamps
3. bed
4. dresser
5. table and chairs
6. boxes
7. dishes
8. silverware
9. clothes
10. desk
11. stove
12. refrigerator
13. rocking chair
14. washer and dryer
15. coffee table

Activity 5

A. Practice reading this letter.

Dear Doris,

Bob and I are happy in our new apartment. We're living on the eighth floor of an old building near the park. We have a nice view of the city.

We also have a good lease. We put down a security deposit and we're paying rent. The security deposit was two hundred dollars and the rent is three hundred and fifty dollars a month. The landlord returns the security deposit at the end of the lease.

There are two bedrooms in the apartment. We're buying a bed and mattress for the extra bedroom. Please visit us! There's plenty of room.

Love,
Jean

B. Write a letter to a relative describing the apartment or house where you live.

Activity 6

A. Practice the conversations.

— We're moving into the neighborhood.
— Are you moving into an apartment?
— No, we're not. We're moving into a house.

— We are signing a lease.
— Are you signing a six-month lease?
— No, we're not. We're signing a one-year lease.

— We are buying furniture.
— Are you buying a bed and dresser?
— No, we're not. We're buying a table and chairs.

— We're moving into a house.
— Are you renting the house?
— No, we're not. We're buying the house.

B. Practice the conversations again, changing **we** to the following:

1. I   4. The Sorianos
2. My parents   5. Julie
3. Jeff   6. Her cousin

Activity 7

A. Take the roles of two tenants and practice the conversations.

Tenant 1: What's the problem?
Tenant 2: The roof is leaking.
Tenant 1: Are you calling the landlord?
Tenant 2: Yes, I am. I'm calling Mr. Birch.

Tenant 1: What's wrong?
Tenant 2: The faucet is leaking.
Tenant 1: Are you calling the water company?
Tenant 2: No, I'm not. I'm calling a plumber.

Tenant 1: What's the problem?
Tenant 2: The water is off.
Tenant 1: Are you calling the landlord?
Tenant 2: No, I'm not. I'm calling the city.

Tenant 1: What's wrong?
Tenant 2: The electricity and gas are off.
Tenant 1: Are you calling the utility company?
Tenant 2: Yes, I am.

B. Take the roles of two tenants in the following situations.

1. The neighbors are noisy.
2. The phone is dead.
3. There's no heat.
4. The plaster is cracking.
5. There are roaches in the kitchen.
6. The disposal doesn't work.
7. The pilot light is off.
8. There's no hot water.

Activity 8

A. Sarah Robertson is calling the telephone company.

Sarah Robertson: Hello. My name is Sarah Robertson. I need a telephone.

Service Representative: What is your address?

Sarah Robertson: It's 790 Sixth Street.

Service Representative: Is it a house?

Sarah Robertson: No. It's an apartment.

Service Representative: Do you want a wall phone?

Sarah Robertson: No. I want a desk phone.

Service Representative: Where do you want the phone?

Sarah Robertson: In the kitchen.

B. Substitute yourself for Sarah Robertson. Ask for a phone installation for your own house or apartment.

UNIT 3

Using Public Services

At the Post Office

Activity 1

A. Practice the conversations, taking the roles of a postal clerk and a customer.

Roberto: I'm going to the post office. I need to mail a letter.

Sara: Good. I'm going there too. I need to buy stamps.

Postal Clerk: Good morning.

Customer: Hello. I need stamps.

Postal Clerk: How many do you need?

Customer: I need a roll of twenty-five-cent stamps.

Postal Clerk: Here you are.

Postal Clerk: May I help you?

Customer: Yes. I want to mail a package.

Postal Clerk: Where are you sending it?

Customer: I'm sending it to New York City. How much is it?

Postal Clerk: It's two dollars and fifty-seven cents.

Customer: I need five aerograms. How much are they?

Postal Clerk: They're thirty-nine cents apiece.

Customer: I want twenty government postcards.

Postal Clerk: Fine. They're fifteen cents each. That's three dollars in all.

Customer: O.K. Here's the money.

Customer: How much is postage for a picture postcard?

Postal Clerk: Are you sending it in the United States?

Customer: Yes, I am.

Postal Clerk: It's fifteen cents.

Customer: How much is postage to Europe?

Postal Clerk: First class is forty-five cents a half ounce. We also have aerograms.

Customer: No, I don't want aerograms. Here are my letters. I want to send them air mail.

B. Take the roles of a postal clerk and a customer who asks:

1. for a book of 25-cent stamps.
2. for five 15-cent stamps.
3. for two government postcards.
4. for a mailing envelope.
5. for seven aerograms.
6. to mail a package to Los Angeles, California.
7. to mail a package containing a book.
8. to insure a package.

Activity 2

A. Practice the conversation, taking the roles of a mother and child.

Child: I want to mail the present to grandma.

Mother: O.K. You need to wrap it with brown paper and postage tape.

Child: What's her address?

Mother: It's 301 Fifth Street, Miami, Florida.

Child: What's the ZIP code?

Mother: It's 33143. You also need the return address.

B. Write your address on a 3″ × 5″ card. Include the ZIP code. Ask each other your addresses and ZIP codes.

C. Exchange 3″ × 5″ cards. Then ask the addresses and ZIP codes of other students (e.g., "What is **his** address?", "What is **their** ZIP code?").

Activity 3

Practice this conversation between a postmaster and a customer, making any necessary changes.

Customer: I want to send a ___A___ .

Postmaster: Where are you sending it?

Customer: I'm sending it to ___B___ . How much is it?

Postmaster: It's ___C___ .

A	B	C
letter	Boulder, Colorado	seventy-five cents
package	Lansing, Michigan	two dollars
postcard	Beaumont, Texas	forty-three cents
money order	Homestead, Florida	eighty-nine cents
aerograms	San Jose, California	a dollar twelve
telegram	Monterrey, Mexico	
	Bangkok, Thailand	
	Calgary, Alberta	
	Carson City, Nevada	

Activity 4

A. Practice reading this information about the post office.

Different Kinds of Mail

The post office has different classes of mail. First class is for letters, personal mail, and packages. First class mail is fast mail. Second class is for magazines. Third class is for advertisements, calendars, and other printed matter. Third class is for light packages, too. There is another class for books. Book rate is slow, but it's not expensive.

The post office sends different types of letters. There are certified, registered, and special-delivery letters. The post office sends a certified letter with regular mail. You receive proof of sending the letter. Registered mail is for valuable letters. The post office insures delivery of the letter. Special-delivery mail arrives quickly. The post office delivers special-delivery letters before other mail.

B. Complete these sentences with your teacher. Then write the answers in your book.

1. Letters, personal mail, and packages

   are _____ class mail.

2. _____ are second class mail.

3. Calendars, advertisements, and light packages

   are _____ class mail.

4. You receive proof of sending a _____

   letter.

5. People send _____ letters by registered

   mail.

6. _____ letters arrive quickly.

Activity 5

Ask the following question by changing the subject and making appropriate changes in the verb. Have another student provide an appropriate answer that specifies the type of mail (e.g., "I'm sending it first class.").

How are _____A_____ sending the $\left\{ \begin{array}{l} \text{letter} \\ \text{package} \end{array} \right.$?

A	Types of Mail
I	first class
you	second class
he	third class
she	book rate
we	certified mail
they	registered mail
	special delivery
	air mail

Activity 6

A. Practice the conversations below.

Postal patron:	I want to send a letter to my aunt in Michigan. What's the ZIP code in Ann Arbor?
Postal clerk:	I don't know. Here's the directory.
Postal patron:	Thank you. Here's Ann Arbor. The ZIP code is 48104.

Customer:	I want to send a money order to my cousin in Mexico.
Currency Exchange clerk:	What's his name?
Customer:	It's Luis Gonzalez.
Currency Exchange clerk:	How much do you want to send?
Customer:	Two hundred dollars.
Currency Exchange clerk:	O.K. There's a fee of a dollar ten. It's $201.10.
Customer:	Fine. Here's the cash.
Currency Exchange clerk:	Thank you. Sign here, please.

B. You are the postal clerk. A customer comes to your window and says:

1. I need to mail this package to Fort Wayne, Indiana.
2. I want to send a money order to my aunt in Conway, South Carolina.
3. I want to send this package book rate. How much is it?
4. I need to mail this letter to Phoenix, Arizona. What's the ZIP code there?
5. I want to send this letter by registered mail.
6. I want to mail a picture postcard to Europe. How much is the postage?

Provide an appropriate answer.

Public Transportation

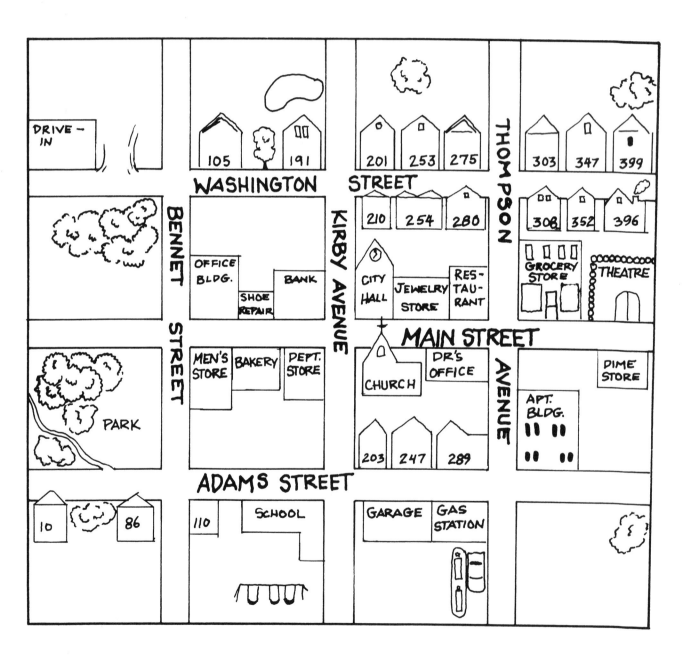

Activity 1

A. Practice these questions and answers. Find the addresses on the city map.

— Where do you live?

— I live on the corner of Adams Street and Bennett Street.

— What's your address?

— It's 86 Adams Street.

— What's your address?

— It's 253 Washington Street.

— Where is it?

— It's between Kirby and Thompson. It's in the middle of the block.

B. Change the addresses in the answers above (e.g., to 247 Adams Street) and alter the directions to fit that address.

C. Ask each other your addresses. Supply other information as in the example. (e.g., It's at the end of the street near the grocery store.)

D. Use the city map to answer each question below. Draw a line between the question and the correct answer:

Where's the garage? ——————————————— It's next to the gas station.

Where's the bakery?   It's at the end of Main Street.

Where's the doctor's office?   It's between the department store and the men's store.

Where's the theater?   It's up the street from the school.

Where's the park?   It's near the church.

Where's the church?   It's on Main Street across from City Hall.

Where's the gas station?   It's across the street from the dime store.

Where's the apartment building?   It's on the corner of Adams Street and Thompson Avenue.

Activity 2

A. Practice these questions and answers.

How do I get to the restaurant?

Go straight on Main Street. It's on the right side of the street.

How do I get to the school?

Turn right on Adams Street. It's on the right side of the street.

How do I get to Washington Street?

Go straight on Kirby Avenue. Cross Adams Street and Main Street. It's the next street after Main Street.

B. Use the map and pretend that you are at the gas station. Ask each other how to get to other places on the map.

C. Ask each other how to get from your classroom to various places within your community. (Note: You may want to use a map of your community as a help.)

Activity 3

A. Using the city map, fill in the missing words in the directions.

Karl: I live in apartment 301.

George: How do I get there?

Karl: Where are you now?

George: I'm at the drive-in.

Karl: O.K. Go _____ on Washington Street

to Thompson Avenue. Turn _____ on

Thompson. Take Thompson Avenue to

_____ Street. The apartment building

is on the corner of _____ Street and

_____ Avenue.

Anita: Meet me at my office.

Bob: O.K. How do I get there?

Anita: Where are you now?

Bob: My address is 399 Washington Street.

Anita: O.K. Take Washington _____ to

Bennett Avenue. Turn _____ on

Bennett. Go to Main _____ . The office

building is on the _____ of Bennett

and Main. I'm in Suite 709. It's on the seventh floor.

Naomi: I need to go to the bank. How do I get there?

Dan: Hmmm . . . We're on the corner of Adams Street and

Bennett _____ . Go

_____ on Bennett to

_____ Street and turn

_____ . The bank is on the

_____ side of the street next to the

_____ store.

José: Come over to my house.

Pam: Where do you live?

José: I live at the end of Adams Street.

Pam: How do I get there?

José: From the apartment building, _____

down Adams _____ . Go past the

school and cross Bennett _____ . It's

the last house on the _____ .

Pam: What's the number?

José: It's number ten.

B. Take the roles of two friends and practice each
conversation.

Activity 4

A. John receives this note at the train station when he arrives in Chicago. Practice reading the note.

John,

Welcome to Chicago! Please take public transportation to my house. I'm on the corner of Clybourn and Webster.

- Go to the subway stop at the corner of State and Madison.
- Take the State Street subway north to the Chicago stop.
- Then take the bus from there. The 44 goes down Clybourn.
- The bus stops at Webster. Get off there.

The fare is a dollar. You don't need exact change on the subway, but you do need a transfer. Transfers are a quarter. Give the transfer to the bus driver. Susan is at home. I arrive at six.

Love,
Ann

B. Answer the following questions.

1. Where is Ann's house?
2. Where is the subway stop?
3. Where does the bus stop?
4. How much is the fare?
5. Does John need exact change?
6. Does he need a transfer?
7. Who is at Ann's house?
8. What time does Ann arrive?

Activity 5

A. Practice these conversations.

— What time is it?
— It's two o'clock.
— What time does the bus arrive?
— At two-oh-five.
— Thank you.

— What time is it?
— It's four forty-five.
— Hmm . . . It's almost time to go.
— Yes. Do you want to have a drink after work?
— No, thanks. Another time. I have to catch the train.
— O.K. See you tomorrow.

— What time does the train leave?
— At six thirty.
— Gee, it's only ten minutes after six. It's here early today.
— Don't worry. It never leaves early. It's always right on time.
— Good! My wife isn't here yet.

— What time is it?
— It's eight thirty.
— Uh-oh. I'm late. I have to hurry.
— What time do you have to be at work?
— At nine o'clock sharp!

— What time do you have?
— It's five to nine.
— Really? I don't believe it! I'm on time!

B. Ask each other the following questions.

1. What time do you get up?
2. What time does your son's school start?
3. When do you arrive at work?
4. When does your boss arrive?
5. When is your lunch hour?
6. What time is it now?
7. When does class end?
8. What time do you leave work?
9. When do your children go to bed?
10. What time does your favorite TV program start?

Activity 6

A. Practice these conversations, taking the roles indicated.

Ben: Are you going home now?

Jay: Yes, I am. Are you?

Ben: Yes. How are you getting there?

Jay: I'm taking the bus. How about you?

Ben: I never take the bus. I always take the subway.

Kay: Where's the bus?

Wendy: It's late.

Kay: That bus is usually on time. What bad luck! Today I'm in a hurry.

Wendy: Don't worry. Here it comes.

Mike: Where are you going for the holidays?

Naomi: I'm going to Denver. My mother lives there.

Mike: How are you going?

Naomi: I'm flying.

Mike: Do you have reservations?

Naomi: Yes, I do.

Customer: I need a ticket to Detroit.

Ticket agent: One way or round trip?

Customer: Round trip, please.

Ticket agent: Smoking or non-smoking?

Customer: Non-smoking. Do you have a window seat?

Ticket agent: Yes, we do. That's fifty-four dollars.

Customer: Here you are.

Ticket agent: Thank you! And have a good trip!

B. Ask and answer the following question, making any necessary changes.

— How do ___A___ get to ___B___ ?

— ___A___ ___C___ take ___D___ .

A	B	C	D
I	work	always	the bus
you	class	never	the car
he	the bank	sometimes	the subway
she	the grocery	usually	the train
we	the city	rarely	the plane
they	the house	frequently	a taxi
		often	

C. Take the role of a customer who calls a reservations clerk and asks for:

1. two round-trip plane tickets to Buffalo, New York.

2. a one-way ticket to Guadalajara, Mexico.

3. an aisle seat in the smoking section on a flight to Washington, D.C.

4. one-way train tickets for two adults and a child to New Orleans, Louisiana.

5. a round-trip train ticket to Boston, Massachusetts, for next Saturday.

Have another classmate be the reservations clerk.

UNIT 4

Communicating with the School

Enrolling a Child in School

Activity 1

A. Practice the conversations, taking the roles indicated.

Mrs. Ramírez:	Hello. I want to enroll my child in school.
Mr. Banks:	Please come in and sit down. I'm Mr. Banks, the principal. What is your name?
Mrs. Ramírez:	I'm Mrs. Ramírez. This is my son, Juan.
Mr. Banks:	Pleased to meet you both. How old are you, Juan?
Juan:	I'm four.
Mrs. Ramírez:	I want to enroll him in kindergarten. What are the requirements?
Mr. Banks:	He has to turn five by December 1st. I need to see a birth certificate.
Mrs. Ramírez:	Good. His birthday is September 29th. I have his birth certificate in my purse.
Mr. Banks:	Good. He also needs an immunization record.

Mother:	What shots does she need?
School secretary:	She needs shots for polio, for measles, and for diphtheria.
Mother:	Does she need a T.B. test?
School secretary:	It's not necessary, but it's a good idea.

Boy: What day does school start?

Girl: It starts on the day after Labor Day.

Boy: What grade are you in?

Girl: I'm in the fifth grade.

Boy: Who's your teacher?

Girl: Mrs. Anderson.

Boy: You're lucky. She was my teacher last year. She's nice.

B. Take the roles of a parent and a principal. Practice enrolling your child in:

1. kindergarten
2. elementary school
3. junior high
4. high school

C. Ask and answer the following questions.

1. What shots does the local school district require?
2. What day does school start?
3. What grade is your son (daughter) in?
4. Who is your child's teacher?
5. Who was your child's teacher last year?

Activity 2

A. In pairs, practice the conversations.

— Who is he?
— He's Mr. Feldman. Last year he was a guidance counselor. Now he's a coach.

— Who's she?
— She's the home economics teacher. Her room is at the end of the hall.

— Who is he?
— That's Mr. Phillips, the choir director. Every year he and the students have a Christmas program. Last year's program was wonderful!

— Who is she?
— That's Ms. Hall, the science teacher. She teaches biology and chemistry.

— Isn't he the math teacher?
— No, he's not. Last year he was the math teacher. This year he teaches gym and driver's education.

B. Ask and answer similar questions about:

1. Ms. Goldsmith, the English teacher.
2. Mr. Schultz, the history teacher.
3. Ms. Wong, the art teacher.
4. Mr. Sharp, the speech teacher.
5. Mrs. Katoaka, the school nurse.
6. Ms. Johnson, the superintendent.

Activity 3

A. Read the parent newsletter.

SEPTEMBER PARENT NEWSLETTER

Summer is over. September is here. The Emerson School is open again. We want to welcome the new members of the faculty. Mrs. Sanchez is the new principal. Last year she was a second grade teacher at Emerson. Mr. Dean is the new second grade teacher. Last year he was a student at the state university. Ms. Chen is the director of the new bilingual program. There are bilingual classes in kindergarten and in grades one through three.

Please visit the Emerson School. All of the faculty at Emerson want to meet you.

B. Answer the following questions.

1. What month is it?
2. Who are the new members of the faculty?
3. Who directs the bilingual program?
4. Who was a student at the state university?

Activity 4

Fill in each blank in the following conversations with one of the word pairs below.

to go	to watch
to behave	to be
to visit	to display
to do	to see

— What time do you get up?

— We always get up early in the morning. My son has

_____ at school at eight o'clock.

_____

— Are you watching the television program?

— No, we aren't. My daughter needs _____
her homework.

_____

— Do you like your child's teacher?

— Yes, very much. The children have _____
in his classroom.

_____

— There's a junior high down the street.

— Yes, I know. We want _____ the school.

— Be sure _____ the art room. The art

teacher likes _____ the students' work.

_____

— How many children do you have?

— We have three children.

— Are they in school?

— Yes. One's in elementary school, one's in junior high, and
one's at the high school. We're lucky. They all like

_____ to school.

_____

— The football team plays a home game this week.

— Yes, I know. Our son is playing. The whole family wants

_____ the game.

LESSON 8

The Role of a Parent

Activity 1

A. Practice the conversation in pairs, taking the parents' roles as indicated.

Mother: We received a note from Sharon's teacher today.

Father: What did she say?

Mother: She wanted to talk to us. Sharon's having problems in reading.

Father: Hmm. That's an important subject. We need to cooperate with the teacher.

Mother: I think so, too. I called the school. I made an appointment for Monday afternoon.

Father: Good.

B. Answer the following questions.

1. What did Sharon's parents receive?
2. What did the teacher say?
3. What did Sharon's mother do?
4. Did you ever receive a note from your child's teacher?

Activity 2

A. Take turns reading this note to Michael's teacher.

> December 11, 1989
>
> Dear Ms. Jones:
>
> Please excuse my son's absence from school on Tuesday and Wednesday. Michael was sick with a cold and a fever. He stayed in bed both days.
>
> Michael is much better now. He wanted to go to school today.
>
> Sincerely,
> (Mrs.) Phyllis Morgan

B. Write a note to your child's teacher, explaining that:

1. Your daughter was absent last week because she had the chicken pox.

2. Your son is recovering from a cold and can't participate in gym class.

3. You have to go out of town to take care of your mother who is ill. You are taking your son with you. He is going to be out of school for three days.

4. Your daughter is home sick with the measles. She is getting better, but she is still contagious.

Activity 3

Practice this conversation in pairs.

— Johnny got his report card today.

— Oh, really? How did he do?

— He got an A in biology and a B+ in English.

— Good. He worked hard during this marking period. He really improved.

Activity 4

A. Practice this conversation in pairs.

Mrs. Sutton: Are you Mrs. Drake?

Mrs. Drake: Yes, I am.

Mrs. Sutton: I'm Mrs. Sutton, Sharon's mother.

Mrs. Drake: Pleased to meet you. Come in and sit down.

Mrs. Sutton: We received your note. My husband and I are concerned about Sharon's progress.

Mrs. Drake: There's no need to worry. Sharon is a good student. She does well in arithmetic. She is always well behaved, but she needs help in reading.

Mrs. Sutton: What do you suggest?

Mrs. Drake: Read to her at home. Take her to the library. The public library has a good children's section. Let her read to you.

Mrs. Sutton: Those are good suggestions.

B. Change the situation and role-play a parent-teacher conference in which the child has a problem in:

1. arithmetic
2. behavior at school
3. speaking English
4. gym class

Activity 5

Change the underlined words to the past tense. Practice the new sentences with your teacher. Write them in your book.

We <u>receive</u> the new adult education schedule yesterday. There <u>are</u> a lot of interesting classes. Miss Stone is teaching the intermediate class of English as a second language this semester. She <u>teaches</u> the beginning class last semester. Mr. Ong <u>takes</u> the GED course last summer. He <u>takes</u> the GED exam in September. He <u>passes</u> the exam. Then he <u>enrolls</u> in a course at the community college. Emilia Navarro <u>goes</u> to a class at the vocational training center. They <u>have</u> a course in auto mechanics last term. They also <u>offer</u> a secretarial course. The schedule <u>lists</u> a lot of recreational courses too.

_____

_____

_____

_____

_____

_____

_____

_____

_____

_____

_____

_____

Activity 6

A. Practice this conversation between two parents.

Parent 1: Did you go to the P.T.A. meeting last night?

Parent 2: Yes, I did. It was interesting.

Parent 1: What happened?

Parent 2: The principal talked about achievement tests. The director of the bilingual program asked parents to volunteer in the classes. And a group of parents had a bake sale to raise money for scholarships.

Parent 1: Did they translate the meeting?

Parent 2: Yes, they did.

B. Change the underlined words to the past tense. Practice the new sentences with your teacher. Then write them in your book.

1. I <u>go</u> to the PTA meeting last night.

   _____

2. It <u>is</u> an informative meeting.

   _____

3. The teachers <u>give</u> achievement tests in September.

   _____

4. Parents <u>volunteer</u> in the bilingual classrooms.

   _____

5. A group <u>raise</u> money for scholarships.

   _____

6. They <u>translate</u> the meeting.

   _____

UNIT 5

Purchasing Clothing

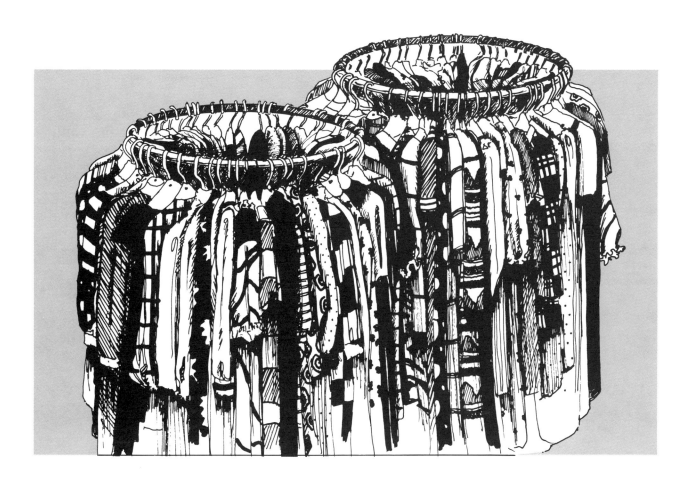

Clothing Needs of the Family

Activity 1

Practice the following conversations between a store clerk and a customer. Substitute other sizes and items of clothing for the underlined words.

Clerk: May I help you?

Customer: Yes. I'm looking for a new <u>dress</u>.

Clerk: What size do you wear?

Customer: I wear a <u>12</u>.

Clerk: The <u>twelves</u> are all on this rack.

Customer: Thank you.

Clerk: Do you like that <u>dress</u>?

Customer: Yes, I do. It's a good style for me and it fits well.

Clerk: Is there anything I can do for you?

Customer: Yes. I'm looking for a <u>shirt</u> to wear with this <u>suit</u>.

Clerk: Do you have something in mind?

Customer: I thought about a <u>gray stripe</u>.

Clerk: That's a good idea. Here's one.

Customer: Mmm. That's nice.

Clerk: Try this <u>tie</u> with it. The colors look nice together.

Clerk: May I help you?

Customer: Yes. I'm looking for <u>slacks</u> and a <u>blouse</u>.

Clerk: What size do you wear?

Customer: A <u>34 blouse</u> and a <u>14</u> in <u>pants</u>.

Clerk: O.K. The separates are over here against the wall.

Activity 2

A. Practice this conversation between a customer and a shoe salesman.

Customer:	I need a new pair of shoes.
Shoe salesman:	What are you looking for?
Customer:	Something to wear to work. A brown leather with a low heel.
Shoe salesman:	Did you see the ones in the window?
Customer:	No, I didn't. They're nice. Let me try them on.
Shoe salesman:	What size do you wear?
Customer:	A 7½ AA. May I try on that pair of sandals, too? They look comfortable.
Shoe salesman:	Certainly.

B. Practice the conversation again, changing the situation to shop for:

1. a dress
2. a man's suit
3. a tie for a Father's Day present
4. a winter coat

Activity 3

A. Taking the roles specified, practice the conversation.

Beth:	What are you doing?
Sue:	I'm putting away my summer clothes and getting out my winter clothes.
Beth:	What's that smell?
Sue:	That's from the mothballs. I put them in my clothes over the summer to protect them.
Beth:	Gee, that's a pretty sweater.
Sue:	Thanks. It goes with this wool skirt.
Beth:	I have to get out my winter clothes too. It *is* getting cold outside!

B. Answer the following questions.

1. What kind of clothes do you wear in the winter?
2. What kind of clothes do you wear in the summer?
3. Do you have special clothes for spring and fall?
4. How do you store your clothes between seasons?

Activity 4

Insert the appropriate words in the blank spaces.

— Don't forget _____ raincoat. It's raining outside.

— Darn! I left _____ umbrella at the office yesterday.

— Here. Take _____ . I'm staying indoors today.

— O.K., thanks! See _____ later.

_____

— That's a pretty nightgown.

— Thanks. But _____ forgot

_____ robe. Do _____ have an extra one?

— Sure. This one belongs to _____ daughter. Try it on. Here are some slippers, too.

— Thanks. _____ robe is fine.

_____ don't need the slippers.

_____ have _____ .

— _____ need some new underwear.

— O.K. Let's go to the department store.

_____ brand is good.

— Why do _____ say that?

— I can put _____ in the washing machine.

_____ last a long time.

— Great! _____ always wear out quickly.

Activity 5

A. Practice the conversation.

Mother: Whose socks are those?

Son: They belong to Ricky.

Daughter: Yep. They're his. He left them there last night.

Mother: Tell him to put them in the laundry basket. And whose gloves are these?

Son: Susie wore them yesterday. They're hers.

Mother: No one in this house ever puts anything away! Whose jacket is that?

Daughter: It belongs to Daddy.

Mother: He has to learn to put things away too!

B. Ask and answer the following questions, changing the nouns and pronouns as needed.

— Whose ___A___ are these?

— They're ___B___ .

A		B
dress	umbrella	yours
coat	boots	his
shoes	earrings	hers
gloves	pajamas	ours
jeans	watch	theirs
		mine

Activity 6

A. Fill in the size chart for yourself and your family.

Size Chart			
Name			
Coat/Suit			
Sweater			
Shoes			
Slacks/Pants			
Shirt/Blouse			
Dress			
Underwear/Lingerie			
Socks			
Birthday			

B. Imagine that you are shopping for clothes for yourself and your family. Practice the following question and answer, changing the subjects and making any necessary changes in the verbs.

Salesperson: What size ___A___ do ___B___ wear?

Customer: ___B___ wear __(size)__.

A
dress
shirt
slacks
blouse
pants
gloves
hat
shoes
suit
socks
coat

B
you
he
she
I
your husband
your wife
your son
your daughter
your mother
your father

Buying Clothing

Activity 1   Practice these conversations. Then answer the questions.

Midge: Where did you get that dress?

Sue: At the women's store on Ramona Street. They have a good selection.

Midge: I never find anything there. I always shop at the department store.

Sue: Why?

Midge: Their clothes usually aren't expensive. And besides, I have their credit card.

1. Where did Sue buy her dress?

2. Why does Midge shop at the department store?

Tom: I lost my wallet.

Alice: Did you lose much money?

Tom: Nope. I never carry much money. But I lost all my credit cards.

Alice: That happened to me last year. Someone stole my purse. I had to cancel all my credit cards. And I had to get new identification.

Tom: That's so much trouble!

Alice: It sure is! Someone found my purse two days later. The money was gone, but the credit cards were there.

1. What did Tom lose?

2. Why did Alice cancel her credit cards?

David: Are those new shoes?

Ann: Yes, they are.

David: Where did you get them?

Ann: At the shoe store on Sixth Street.

David: Why did you buy them there?

Ann: I have a long, narrow foot. Many stores don't carry my size. That store always has a number of styles in a 9½ narrow.

David: That's good to know. I need some new winter boots. I didn't like the ones at the department store, but I didn't look at other stores.

1.   Where did Ann buy her shoes?

2.   What does David need?

Mrs. Hutton: Look at the new suits!

Ms. Miranda: Gee, they're nice. I like the material.

Mrs. Hutton: Why don't you try one on?

Ms. Miranda: O.K. This one is a pretty color.

Mrs. Hutton: That suit looks nice on you. Why don't you get it?

Ms. Miranda: I don't have the money right now.

Mrs. Hutton: Put it on layaway. You just have to pay a deposit.

Ms. Miranda: That's a good idea.

1.   What does Ms. Miranda like?

2.   Does she buy a suit?

Activity 2

Change these sentences to the simple past tense.

1. The shoe store carries that brand.

   _____

2. He pays cash for everything.

   _____

3. We shop at the department store.

   _____

4. I need to cancel my credit cards.

   _____

5. They pay a deposit.

   _____

6. The woman charges her purchases.

   _____

7. My father applies for a credit card.

   _____

8. The clothing store carries my size.

   _____

9. We buy the furniture on credit.

   _____

10. She puts the coat on layaway.

   _____

Activity 3

A. Taking the roles specified, practice the conversation.

Husband: The monthly bill from the department store came today.

Wife: How much was it?

Husband: Around a hundred and thirty dollars.

Wife: That's really high.

Husband: Yes, but we bought most of our Christmas presents there.

Wife: You're right. I forgot about that.

Husband: Let's pay the bill by the end of the month.

Wife: Why?

Husband: The finance charge is 18 percent on the unpaid balance.

B. Answer the following questions.

1. What arrived today?
2. Where did the couple buy their Christmas presents?
3. When did they plan to pay the bill?
4. How much is the finance charge?

Activity 4

A. Read the following passage.

INFORMATION ABOUT YOUR BANK CARD—DID YOU KNOW . . . ?

- Finance charges for the year appear on your December statement. Please keep this statement with all others for your records.

- Please keep all copies of receipts for your bank card purchases. Check these copies against your statement.

- Your credit limit appears on your monthly statement.

- Do you want to increase your credit limit? Please contact our office for additional information.

- Additional cards for members of your family are available.

- Did you lose your credit card? Keep a record of your credit card number at home. Report a lost credit card to our office immediately.

- Our bank card staff is happy to serve you. Our toll-free telephone number is 1-800-555-0741.

B. Complete these sentences with your teacher. Then fill in the blanks in your book.

1. You receive your _____ charges for the year in the month of _____ .

2. Keep all copies of _____ and check them against your _____ .

3. Contact the _____ for information on how to _____ your credit limit.

4. A person's credit _____ appears on every _____ .

5. You need to _____ a lost credit card to the _____ immediately.

6. The toll-free number is _____ .

Activity 5

A. Practice the conversations, taking the roles indicated.

Maria: How much did you pay for that sweater?

Guy: Eighteen dollars plus tax.

Maria: Oh, really? What's the sales tax in this state?

Guy: Five cents on the dollar.

Maria: Is there a tax on everything?

Guy: No, there's no tax on food. But there's a luxury tax on liquor and cigarettes.

Maria: How much is that?

Guy: Eight cents on the dollar. The tax money goes toward the state's educational system.

B. Answer the following questions in class discussion.

1. Is there a sales tax in your state?
2. How much is it?
3. What does the state do with the money?
4. In your state, is there a tax on

   a. food?   b. liquor?   c. cigarettes?

5. How much is your sales tax on a purchase of

   a. $18.00?   c. $7.06?   e. $9.98?
   b. $3.45?   d. $25.25?   f. $30.66?

UNIT 6

Dealing with Money

Setting Up a Budget

Activity 1

A. Practice this conversation, taking the roles of the husband and wife.

> Wife: These bills are too high. We need to set up a budget.
>
> Husband: Why? How much did we spend last month?
>
> Wife: I don't know. That's the problem!
>
> Husband: Well, this is the end of the month. It's a good time to make a budget.
>
> Wife: I agree. Let's do it tonight.

B. Answer the following questions.

1. How much did the couple spend last month?
2. How much did you spend last month?
3. Do you have a budget?

Activity 2

Change **this** to **that** or **that** to **this** as you substitute the new word for the underlined word.

EXAMPLE:

This is the <u>problem</u>.   (solution)
That is the solution.

1. This expense is <u>unreasonable</u>.   (reasonable)

2. That is a <u>bad</u> time to make a budget.   (good)

_____

3. This expense was <u>planned</u>.   (unexpected)

_____

4. This bill is <u>low</u>.   (high)

_____

5. That is a <u>long</u> list.   (short)

_____

6. We allowed <u>two hundred</u> dollars for that item.
   (a thousand)

_____

Activity 3

A. Practice this conversation, taking the roles of the husband and wife from Activity 1.

Wife: How do we start?

Husband: Let's make a list of our expenses. For example, our major expenses are housing and food.

Wife: We also spend money on clothing and utilities.

Husband: Don't forget to include gasoline, repairs, and insurance.

Wife: There are lots of other expenses, too. We spend money on doctor bills, laundry, and things for the house.

Husband: We have to think about recreation, too. We spend money on movies and babysitters.

Wife: That's a long list!

B. Answer the following questions.

   1. What are the couple's major expenses?
   2. What are your major expenses?

Activity 4

Change **these** to **those** and **those** to **these** as you substitute the new word for the underlined word.

EXAMPLE:

Those are <u>unnecessary</u> purchases.   (necessary)

These are necessary purchases.

   1. These are the <u>necessities</u>.   (extras)

   _____

   2. Those bills are for <u>food</u>.   (housing)

   _____

   3. I <u>paid</u> those bills.   (didn't pay)

   _____

   4. These items are <u>deductible</u>.   (not deductible)

   _____

   5. Those are <u>transportation</u> expenses.   (medical)

   _____

   6. He bought these <u>clothes</u> on credit.   (appliances)

   _____

Activity 5

A. Practice the conversation.

Husband: What do we do next?

Wife: First, we need to know our income. Then we need to plan our expenses for each item on our list.

Husband: O.K. You earn $900 a month. My salary is $750 a month. That's $1650 a month in all.

Wife: Don't forget to subtract taxes. We really have about $1300 to spend.

Husband: Most people spend about one-fourth of their income for housing. Our rent is $375. That's a reasonable amount.

Wife: We spend about $75 a week for food. That's $300 a month.

Husband: The other items on the budget are more difficult. We need to estimate those expenses.

Wife: Don't forget to plan for savings.

B. Plan monthly budgets based on the following amounts. Include expenses for housing, food, transportation, clothes, utilities, recreation, and savings.

1. $1,500 a month
2. $700 a month
3. $900 a month
4. $1,200 a month

Activity 6

Change each sentence from positive to negative or from negative to positive, as shown in the example.

EXAMPLE:

You went over the budget there.
You didn't go over the budget there.

1. He spent one fourth of his income for rent.

   _____

2. We didn't forget to include medical expenses in the budget.

   _____

3. This month they stayed within their food budget.

   _____

4. He didn't plan to buy a new car.

   _____

5. I needed to adjust the budget for vacation.

   _____

6. She didn't spend all of her salary.

   _____

7. We forgot to include recreation in the budget.

   _____

8. Last month they didn't stay within their clothing budget.

_____

9. She planned to spend $25 on a dress.

_____

10. I didn't need to spend money on clothes last month.

_____

Activity 7

A. Practice the conversation in pairs.

Wife: How did we do on our budget this month?

Husband: I'm not sure. We stayed under the budget on some things. But we went over the budget on other things.

Wife: Let's look at the bills.

Husband: O.K. We didn't go over the budget on housing. But we didn't stay within the budget on food.

Wife: We didn't allow enough in the budget for food. Prices went up this month.

Husband: You're right.

Wife: The phone bill was high, too.

Husband: That long-distance call to Ohio was an unnecessary expense.

Wife: Also, we went over the budget on the car. That car repair was an unexpected expense.

Husband: But we didn't go over the budget on clothing or on recreation. And we didn't spend anything on medical bills.

Wife: We came out even this month. We need to adjust our budget for next month.

B. Answer the following questions.

1. How did you do on your budget this month?

2. Did you have any unnecessary expenses?

3. Did you have any unexpected expenses?

4. Did you go over your budget on any expenses?

Activity 8

A. Read these suggestions.

MONEY-SAVING SUGGESTIONS

Did you spend too much last month? Did you stay within your budget?
No? Try these suggestions:

1. Cut some items from your budget; spend less for some items.
2. Use your skills. (Wash your car. Make your own clothes.) Don't pay other people to do those things.
3. Don't eat lunch in a restaurant. Bring your lunch from home.
4. Use free community services. Many communities have libraries, recreation centers, parks, and other services. These are free to the public.
5. Look for specials at the grocery store.
6. Get information about products from Consumer Guides.
7. Buy used furniture.
8. Compare prices.
9. Look for quality.
10. Look for sales.
11. Learn about credit purchases. Avoid finance charges.
12. Use a shopping list.

B. Are any of these suggestions helpful? If so, which ones?

C. Can you think of other suggestions?

Using the Bank

Activity 1

A. Practice this conversation, taking the roles of a bank teller and a customer.

Teller: May I help you?

Customer: Yes. I want to open a checking account.

Teller: O.K. We have two kinds of accounts. One has free checking. But you have to keep a minimum balance of $200. The other requires no minimum balance. The fee is 25¢ a check.

Customer: I don't want to keep a minimum balance. I'll pay for the checks.

Teller: Will you make a deposit now?

Customer: Yes, I will.

Teller: How much?

Customer: I'll deposit $500.

B. Answer the following questions.

1. What does the person want to do at the bank?
2. What is a minimum balance?
3. How much is the minimum balance on the free checking account?
4. How much is the fee on the other account?
5. Which account does the man want?
6. How much is the fee for six checks?

Activity 2

A. Practice the sentences that describe the following pictures.

I'll write a check.

She'll cash a check.

We'll open a checking account.

They'll open a savings account.

You'll pay cash.

He'll pay by check.

Richard and I will make a deposit.

They'll make a withdrawal.

B. Change the sentences to questions.

C. Answer the questions.

Activity 3

A. In pairs, practice the conversation.

Fred: When will you go to the bank?

Alma: I'll go to the bank on Monday morning.

Fred: Why?

Alma: I'm out of cash. I'll need some money for the week.

Fred: O.K. I'll cash a check for you. How much will you need?

Alma: I'll need $50.

Fred: All right. I'll try to remember.

B. Change the situation so that:

1. She will go to the bank on Wednesday afternoon.
2. He needs $75.
3. He wants her to deposit his paycheck.
4. She needs to withdraw $30 from the savings account.

C. Answer the following questions using the words supplied here. Then practice answering the questions in your own words.

1. When will they go to the bank?   (on Friday)
2. What will she want?   (some cash)
3. How much will you need?   ($14)
4. Who will be your teller?   (Mr. Hansen)

Activity 4

A. Practice writing a check to Riverside Gas Company for $25.00.

FIRST NATIONAL BANK   235

Barbara Graham
1727 Walnut Street   8-12
Pittsburgh, PA 15212   19   ―――
                                                      430

Pay to the
Order of _____ $ _____

_____ Dollars

First National Bank
Pittsburgh, Pennsylvania 15212

Memo

⑆0430⑈0012⑆ 12⑈345674⑈

B. Now write out these amounts as you would write them on a check.

1. $37.59

   _____

2. $66.34

   _____

3. $127.11

   _____

Activity 5

A. In pairs, practice this conversation.

Customer: I want to cash a check.

Teller: Do you have an account with this bank?

Customer: Yes, I do. The account number is 325406.

Teller: Will you endorse this check, please?

Customer: Sure.

Teller: Do you want anything special?

Customer: Yes. I want a twenty, two tens, and two fives.

B. Answer the following questions.

1. What is your checking account number?
2. Is your account number on your checks?
3. What is your savings account number?
4. Is your savings account number on your passbook?

Activity 6   Draw a line between each question and its answer.

Will you pay cash?	Yes, they will. They'll include the deposit slip and the endorsed checks.
Will you make a deposit?	Yes, I will. I'll take out $30.
Will you go to the bank?	No, they won't. They'll bank by mail.
Will you endorse the check, please?	Yes, I will. I'll sign it on the back.
Will you open a joint account?	No, I won't. I'll wait to buy the furniture.
Will you open a savings account?	Yes, I will. I'll deposit my paycheck.
Will you go inside the bank?	No, I won't. I'll balance the checkbook.
Will you make a withdrawal?	Yes, I will. I'll open a passbook account.
Will you overdraw the account?	No, I won't. I'll go to the drive-in window.
Will they include the deposit slip?	No, I won't. I'll write a check.
Will you take out a loan?	No, we won't. We'll open two single accounts.
Will they go to the bank?	No, I won't. I'll go to the currency exchange.

Activity 7

A. In pairs, practice the conversation.

Husband: What are you going to do?

Wife: I'm going to balance the checkbook.

Husband: Already? We just received the bank statement.

Wife: Yes. But we overdrew the account last month. I don't want to do that again.

Husband: You're right! What will you need?

Wife: I'll need the checkbook and the canceled checks. I'll also want to use the calculator.

B. Answer the following questions.

1. What is the woman going to do?
2. What will she need?
3. What happened last month?
4. Will it happen this month?

Activity 8

A. Practice the conversation, taking the roles of a bank teller and a customer.

Customer: I want to make a withdrawal from my savings account.

Teller: Do you have your passbook with you?

Customer: Yes, here it is.

Teller: How much do you want to withdraw?

Customer: I'll take out $200.

Teller: Do you want that in cash?

Customer: No, thanks. Will you give me a certified check, please?

Teller: Certainly. Just a minute. I'll give you your check and I'll return your passbook with the new balance.

B. Practice the conversation again, changing the situation to make

    1. a deposit in the savings account

    2. a withdrawal of $450

    3. a deposit into the checking account

    4. the same withdrawal but you, as the customer, left the passbook at home

Activity 9

A. In pairs, practice this conversation between a loan officer and someone applying for a loan.

Loan officer: What can I do for you?

Applicant: I want to apply for a loan.

Loan officer: How much money will you need?

Applicant: My family is moving across the country. I'll need $950 for moving expenses.

Loan officer: O.K. Will you fill out this application, please?

Applicant: Sure. When will I know your decision?

Loan officer: We'll need to check your credit rating. I'll call you at work on Friday.

Applicant: Good. Thanks for your help.

B. Practice the conversation again, changing the situation to ask for a loan

    1. of two thousand dollars

    2. to buy a car

    3. to put a down payment on a house

    4. to pay for your child's college expenses

UNIT 7

Purchasing and Maintaining an Automobile

LESSON 13

Buying a Car

Activity 1

A. In pairs, practice this conversation between a customer and a car salesman.

Salesman: Hello. May I help you?

Customer: I'm looking for a new car.

Salesman: What do you have in mind.

Customer: I heard about your new economy car.

Salesman: There's one on the other side of the showroom. Do you want to see it?

Customer: Sure.

Salesman: Here it is. It has an automatic shift. There are two-door and four-door models.

Customer: What kind of gas mileage does it get?

Salesman: Thirty miles to the gallon on the highway and twenty-five in the city.

Customer: Terrific! May I take it for a test drive?

Salesman: Certainly.

B. Answer the following questions.

1. Does the customer want a big car?

2. Does the car have a standard shift?

3. Does the car get the same mileage on the highway and in the city?

4. Does the salesman take the car for a test drive?

Activity 2

Use a question-and-answer drill to practice asking for accessories on your new car. As you answer the question, repeat the accessory the previous person(s) said and add your own, using the words supplied in Column B or supplying the name of another accessory.

1st Person: What kind of car do you want?

2nd Person: I want a ____A____ .
What kind of car do you want?

3rd Person: I want a ____A____ with ____B____.
What kind of car do you want? (etc.)

A		B
two-door model	a radio	a heater
four-door sedan	whitewall tires	bucket seats
compact car	radial tires	air conditioning
station wagon	an automatic shift	a black interior
hatchback	a standard shift	a tape deck
	power steering	

Activity 3

A. Practice the conversation, taking the roles of a customer and a used car salesman.

Customer: I'm in the market for a used car.

Salesman: Are you looking for something in particular?

Customer: Well, I prefer a small car. And it has to be reliable.

Salesman: There are two compact cars on the lot. One is a 1984 and the other is a 1986. Both are in good condition.

Customer: How many miles do they have on them?

Salesman: The 1986 has sixty thousand miles. The 1984 only has ten thousand miles.

Customer: Why is that?

Salesman: It was a second car. The owner rarely drove it.

Customer: That one sounds like a better deal. May I see it?

Salesman: Sure.

B. Answer the following questions.

1. Will you buy a car this year?
2. Will you buy a new car?
3. What kind of car will you buy?
4. What kind of gas mileage do you want?

Activity 4

A. Study these diagrams and learn the parts of a car.

1. rear view mirror
2. seat belt
3. windshield
4. windshield wiper
5. hood
6. grille
7. headlight

8. license plate
9. bumper
10. tire
11. hub cap
12. front door
13. door handle

14. rear door
15. gas cap
16. trunk lid
17. rear window
18. side window

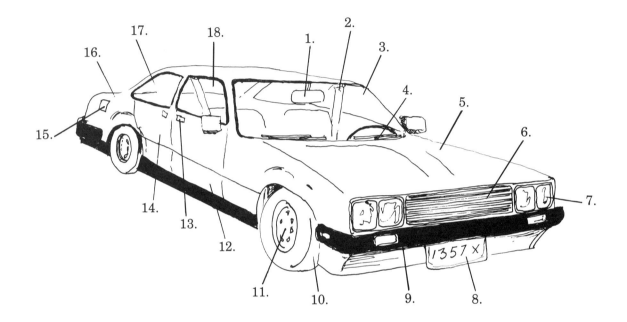

19. battery
20. radiator
21. engine/motor
22. front wheel
23. brake pedal
24. clutch pedal
25. gear shift

26. steering wheel
27. front seat
28. back seat
29. rear wheel
30. gas tank
31. spare tire
32. trunk
33. gas pedal

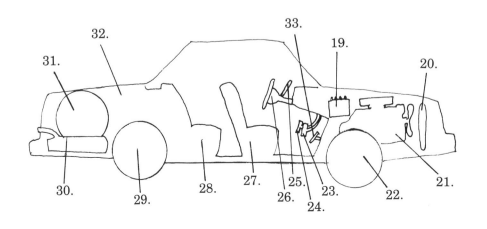

B. Fill in the blanks with parts of a car from the diagrams. Make any necessary changes. You may use each part more than once.

1. His right rear _____ is flat. Does he have a _____ ?

2. I accidentally left the _____ at the gas station. I need to replace it.

3. The driver always sits in the

   _____ .

4. I always need to adjust the _____ when I drive someone else's car.

5. He backed into a fire hydrant and put a dent in the

   _____ .

6. The _____ is a safe place for the baby's car seat.

7. The gas station attendant sometimes cleans the

   _____ .

8. The boys stole the _____ from the parked car.

9. They make _____ at the state prison.

10. Always turn on the _____ in the rain.

11. Always wear a _____ . It's safe. And it's the law in many states.

12. My husband left the _____ on. He

    ran down the _____ .

13. The mechanic opened the _____

    to work on the _____ .

14. Always push in the _____ to change gears.

Activity 5

Insert these words in the sentences that follow. You may use a word more than once.

always   usually
never   frequently
every 3,000 miles   once in a while
once a week   rarely
regularly   occasionally
every three months often
once a year

1. You need to change your oil

   _____ .

2. I _____ check the oil and water at the gas station.

3. _____ go on a trip without checking the treads on your tires.

4. I get a tune-up _____ .

5. He checks his brakes _____ .

6. She _____ carries battery cables in her car.

7. I fill up with gas _____ .

8. _____ use the same brand of oil.

9. You need to put antifreeze in your car

   _____ .

10. I _____ check my tire pressure before a trip.

11. In the winter they _____ had to charge their battery.

12. _____ the gas station attendants will check your oil and water for you.

13. I check the water in my battery

_____ .

14. _____ he buys premium gasoline.

15. I _____ depend on my mechanic for minor repairs.

16. I look at my indicator lights quite

_____ .

17. _____ carry a spare tire.

18. I _____ need new windshield wipers.

Activity 6

A. In pairs, practice this conversation between a customer and a car salesman.

Customer: I want to trade in my old car. What will you give me for it?

Salesman: What kind of a car is it?

Customer: It's a 1984 Ford station wagon.

Salesman: How many miles are on it?

Customer: About eighty thousand miles. But the engine runs well and it has new brakes.

Salesman: You're right. The car is in good condition. But it needs new tires and a paint job. We can give you $800 for it.

B. Practice the conversation again, changing the car to

1. a 1986 Toyota Tercel
2. a 1980 Chevrolet sedan with new tires
3. a 1985 Buick with rust spots and only 2,000 miles on it
4. a 1987 Volkswagen Rabbit in perfect condition

Activity 7

A. Practice reading this insurance information.

AUTOMOBILE INSURANCE

It is a good idea to have insurance on your car. Accidents happen unexpectedly. They are often expensive. An insurance policy helps you pay for the damage.

There are many different kinds of coverage. You need to choose your policy wisely. Insurance companies offer coverage for bodily injury to others, for personal injury, and for medical payments. They also have coverage for property damage and collision coverage. There is coverage to protect you from the uninsured motorist. Comprehensive coverage is for theft, fire, or vandalism. Sometimes you have to pay a deductible.

In many states, car owners have to buy auto insurance. Other states do not require car insurance. You need to know the requirements for car insurance in your state.

B.   Draw a line between the situation and the coverage you need.

1.   You are driving your car. You are in an accident. You and your passengers are hurt. You have to pay hospital bills. You need _____ .

2.   You are driving your car. You are in an accident. One of your passengers is hurt. You need _____ .

3.   You are in an accident. There is damage to your car. You have to pay the body shop to repair it. You need _____ .

4.   You are driving your car. You are in an accident and you are hurt. You need _____ .

5.   You leave your car in the parking lot at work overnight. Someone breaks into the car, drives it to a nearby town, breaks the windshield, and steals some parts. You need to pay for the repairs. You need _____ .

6.   You are in an accident. There is $800 worth of damage to your car. Your insurance company will pay $700. You have to pay the first $100. You have to pay a _____ .

7.   You are in an accident with another car. The accident is the other person's fault. The other driver does not have insurance. You need _____ .

8.   You are in an accident. You damage another person's property. That person wants you to pay for the damage. You need _____ .

a.   bodily injury to others

b.   personal injury

c.   medical payments

d.   property damage

e.   collision coverage

f.   uninsured motorist

g.   comprehensive coverage

h.   deductible

Driving a Car

Activity 1

A. Practice this conversation, taking the roles of a driver's license examiner and an applicant for a driver's license.

License examiner:	May I help you?
Applicant:	Yes. I want to apply for a driver's license.
License examiner:	Did you take a driver's education class?
Applicant:	Yes, I did. I have a learner's permit.
License examiner:	Okay. First you need a vision test. Can you read this line?
Applicant:	Yes, I can. T Z V E C F.
License examiner:	Next you need to take a written test. Now you have to take a road test. (time passes)
License examiner:	Can you parallel park?
Applicant:	Yes, I can. Here's a space.
License examiner:	You passed the tests. We'll mail your license to you within a month. You can drive on this permit until then.

B. Answer the following questions.

1. Do you have a driver's license?
2. Did you take driver's education?
3. Can you pass a vision test without glasses?
4. Can you parallel park?
5. Did you take a written test?
6. Did you have to take a road test?

Activity 2

A. Practice reading the following information.

Traffic Signs

The shape of a road sign gives you important information.

An eight-sided sign means **stop.**
You must stop at a stop sign.

A triangular sign means **yield.**
You must slow down and let
other cars go first.

A round sign tells you about
a nearby **railroad crossing.**
You should stop and look for
a train.

A diamond-shaped sign gives you
a **warning**. You should pay
attention to these signs.

A rectangular sign gives you
information. You must obey
the signs.

Watch for signs whenever you drive. They help you to drive safely.

B. What do signs with the following shapes mean?

1. round   _____
2. octagon   _____
3. rectangle   _____
4. triangle   _____
5. diamond   _____

Activity 3

A. In pairs, practice the following conversation.

Applicant: I need to get license plates for my car.

Clerk: May I see your registration, please?

Applicant: I don't have it with me.

Clerk: You can't get license plates without it. We need to see three things: your registration, your title, and your inspection certificate.

Applicant: O.K. I'll get them. I'll come back in an hour.

Clerk: You should wait until tomorrow. We close at five o'clock.

B. Answer the following questions.

1. What does the applicant need to get his license plates?

2. What must you have to get license plates in your state?

3. Where can you buy your license plates?

4. When is the office open?

Activity 4

Fill in the blanks with **should**, **should not**, **may**, **may not**, **must**, and **must not**. Choose the best answer for each sentence.

1. You _____ wear your seat belt.

2. You _____ go on a green light.

3. You _____ drive on the right side of the street.

4. You _____ park next to a fire hydrant.

5. You _____ stop at a railroad crossing.

6. You _____ drive on the left side of the street.

7. You _____ cross a solid double line.

8. You _____ proceed with caution on a yellow light.

9. You _____ pass another car on a hill.

10. You _____ obey traffic signs.

11. You _____ make a U turn on a one-way street.

12. You _____ stop at a red light.

13. You _____ drive fast in the rain.

14. You _____ go over the speed limit.

15. You _____ park next to an open meter.

16. You _____ turn right on red without stopping.

17. You _____ use your headlights at night.

18. You _____ cross a solid line in your lane to pass.

19. You _____ stop for a school bus.

20. You _____ cross a broken line to pass.

21. You _____ signal before a turn.

22. You _____ pass another car on the right.

Activity 5

A. In pairs, practice this conversation between a customer and a gas station attendant.

Attendant: What can I do for you?

Customer: Fill it up with regular.

Attendant: O.K. Do you want me to check under the hood?

Customer: Please. And would you clean the windshield for me, too, please?

Attendant: Sure. Eight gallons. That'll be $8.80. Cash or credit card?

Customer: It'll be cash.

B. Practice the conversation again, changing the situation so that the customer

1. buys self-serve gasoline
2. asks for an oil change
3. pays with a credit card
4. buys unleaded gas

Activity 6

A. Practice reading these suggestions from an insurance company.

IN CASE OF AN AUTOMOBILE ACCIDENT

Follow these steps:
1. Stop immediately.
2. Keep calm.
3. Warn oncoming traffic.
4. Get license number and names of persons involved and of witnesses.
5. Call the police.
6. Make an accident report to the police.
7. Call your insurance agent.
8. Do not talk about the accident with anyone except the police and your insurance agent.

B. Role-play a minor automobile accident using these suggestions.

Activity 7

A. In pairs, practice this conversation between a police officer and a driver.

Police officer: May I see your driver's license, please?

Driver: Here it is, officer. What's the problem?

Police officer: You're driving too fast. And you ran a red light.

Driver: Where? I didn't see it.

Police officer: You should slow down. It was at that last corner.

Driver: I'm sorry, officer. I won't do it again.

Police officer: Good. You could hurt someone that way. Here's your ticket. You have to be in court on Monday.

Driver: All right, officer. I'll be there.

B. Practice the conversation again, changing the situation so that the driver

1. left his license at home

2. was under the influence of alcohol

3. was driving with only one headlight

4. was taking his wife to the hospital to have a baby

5. is unable to be in court on Monday. He has to be at work in another town 200 miles away

UNIT 8

Finding a Job

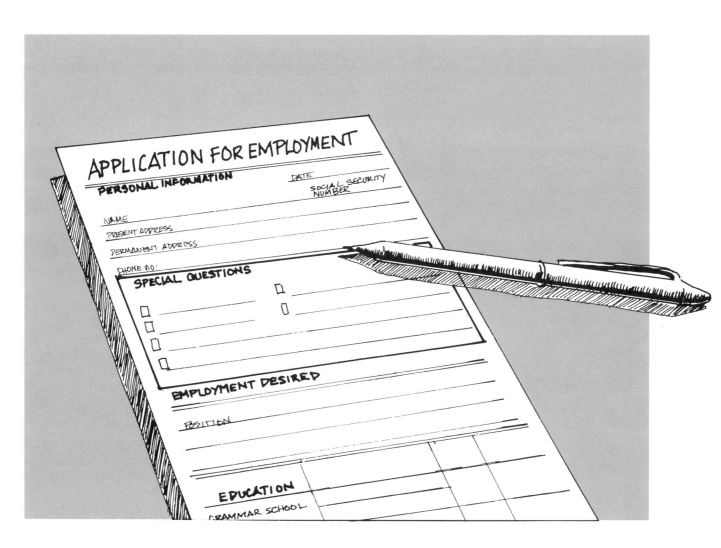

LESSON 15

Identifying a Job

Activity 1

A. In pairs, practice this conversation.

Man: What are you doing?

Neighbor: I'm looking for a job.

Man: Don't you already have a job?

Neighbor: Yes, I do. But I want a better job. I need more money.

Man: What kind of work are you looking for?

Neighbor: I want a mechanic's job. Mechanics earn better wages than I do.

Man: Do you have experience?

Neighbor: Yes, I do. I worked as a mechanic for two years before I moved here.

Man: Are there any openings for mechanics?

Neighbor: Yes, there are. The paper has several ads for mechanics.

B. Answer the following questions.

1. Do you have a job?
2. Do you want a better job?
3. What kind of work do you want?
4. Are there enough openings for that kind of work?

Activity 2

Change the underlined words in the sentences below.

EXAMPLE:

The Sunday paper has <u>more</u> want ads.

The Sunday paper has <u>the most</u> want ads.

1. They give you <u>better</u> advice at the state employment service.

   _____

2. I have <u>less</u> experience as a carpenter.

   _____

3. The boss earns a <u>higher</u> salary.

   _____

4. My new job is <u>more</u> interesting.

   _____

5. That employment agency charges you a <u>bigger</u> fee.

   _____

6. The factory job requires <u>fewer</u> years of experience.

   _____

7. It takes him <u>less</u> time to get to work.

   _____

8. The battery shop is a <u>smaller</u> business.

_____

9. This newspaper has <u>newer</u> job listings.

_____

10. In the spring, the company has a <u>greater</u> need for new employees.

_____

Activity 3

A. In pairs, practice this telephone conversation between a job applicant and an interviewer.

Caller: I'm calling about the ad for a bookkeeper. I want to make an appointment for an interview.

Interviewer: Do you have experience as a bookkeeper?

Caller: Yes, I do. I worked as a bookkeeper in a hospital for a year and a half.

Interviewer: How fast do you type?

Caller: I type 55 words per minute.

Interviewer: Good. I'd like to talk with you. Could you come in for an interview at 9:30 on Monday morning?

Caller: Yes, I could. That's a good time for me.

Interviewer: Fine. I'll see you at 9:30.

Caller: Good. Thank you very much. Goodbye.

B. Practice the conversation again, changing the situation so that the caller

1. is answering an ad for a secretary

2. cannot go in for the interview on Monday because she has to work

3. does not have the qualifications for the job

4. is answering an ad for a telephone operator

Activity 4

A. Read these want ads for jobs. Make sure you understand the meanings of any abbreviations you see. Use the list of want-ad abbreviations in the appendix for help.

DENTAL HYGIENEST(S) wanted full & PT for busy NW Chgo. office. Full schedule already booked! 555-1500.

DENTAL ASSISTANT
Full-time dental assist. wanted. Exp. only Lincoln Pk. 555-4524

DESK CLERK
For Northside rooming house. Must be aggressive. 555-0850.

DIE CUTTER
Must be able to make ready and operate platten die cutting press, and move own stock. Will train to operate programmed paper cutter. High school graduate with at least 2 years experience. Good salary with many co. benefits.
MACO ART INDUSTRIES
1832 Juneway Terr.
Chgo (nr. Howard & Clark)
555-3430

DOCKWORKER TRAINEE
See #095 emply svc 555-1848 Access 1 Job Ref'l Svc $75

DRAFTSPERSON with 2-4 years experience for North Michigan Ave. commercial and retail architectural firm. Call 555-3355 ask for Ben.

DRAPERY SEAMSTRESS
MUST BE EXPERIENCED
Call 555-3234

DRIVERS-VENDING ROUTE
Opening for drivers with good driving records. Vending exp. preferred, but not necessary. Other route experience acceptable. Must be reliable and honest, able to pass polygraph. Excellent starting salary, company benefits and profit-sharing. Apply in person, 8 A.M. to 2 P.M.
Kinney Food Systems
12633 S. Springfield
Alsip, IL 60658
(2 Blks E. of Crawford)

DRIVERS: IT'S GREAT TO BE AT BTS-EARN UP TO $35,000 OR MORE. BTS OFFERS:
.25¢ per mile bonus, $100 min. pay, unloading/loading pay, drop pay, new equipment, company paid insurance, paid vacation, stock purchase plan, 2 years OTR verifiable exp. req. Apply at 815-555-2382.

DRIVERS
People needed to deliver books to offices and businesses. No experience necessary. We pay $500/week. Neat appearance and own car essential. Apply in person, 1782 Newport Dr, Unit 6, Rolling Meadows, IL

DRIVERS-PIZZA
Work for Chicago's top pizzeria. $6 + /hr. Full or part-time. 555-0829, call after 4:30 pm.

DRY CLEANING
Manager for busy dry cleaning plant counter. FT-6 days. PM shift. Must be exp with references. Top pay & more.
Call 555-9636 before 10am.

SALES
Sales of bldg. materials to architects, builders and contractors. Well established co. has a rare opportunity for an aggressive self-motivated salesperson looking for a career oppty. Exp. helpful but not necessary. Salary, comm., allowance, insurance avail. Send letter or resume to P.O. Box 803883, M8801 Chicago, Il. 60680

SALES TRAINEE
Opportunity for the right person . . . . Call 555-2988

SECRETARY EXEC LEGAL
★★$28,500★★
Dynamic Real Estate Partner
Assist dynamic real estate partner in/out of court. Heavy client contact. Must have excellent appearance, good skills and like people. No pressure. Single assignment only. Wonderful benefits. Call Sharon Taylor 9am-9pm 555-2288

Secretary
WORD PROCESSING
$20,000-$22,000
Use your W/P and secretarial skills while interacting with all corporate levels. Much variety. Great client benefits. Call Sun. 1-4 and Weekdays: 555-7200

SECRETARY/EXECUTIVE
Experienced, well organized, detail minded person. Must have exc. communication skills & good grammar. Typing 60 + & shorthand req. WP a plus. Send resume & salary requirements in confidence to: Dept. CP, REV, 400 N. Michigan Ave., Chicago IL 60611

★★★★★★★★★★★★
SEWING MACHINE OPERATOR
Must be able to handle 200 pound rolls of material for cutting and sewing. Must be exper. on industrial sewing machine. Full time year round work. Must speak English. No smoking. Halsted/Belmont.555-9622 Mr. Ross
★★★★★★★★★★★★

STEEL PERSON Exp. in warehouse mgmt., sales, must have knowledge of secondary steel, Gary IN. Call Teri Matthews collect 1-609-555-8920.

SWITCHBOARD OPERATOR/ RECEPTIONIST
Merchandise Mart design firm looking for an experienced professional switchboard operator/receptionist. Call 555-8937.

TAILOR/FITTER
Full and part time. Hours flex. Good pay. Chicago, Prospect Heights & Darien CALL FOR APPOINTMENT. TJ TAILORS 555-1178

TYPESETTING
Full-time position available for accurate typist. Min. 50 wpm. Exp. helpful but will train right person. Other duties will include paste up and proofreading. Call 555-6100 for an appt. Applications being taken 9am-12 noon, 2337 S. Laramie Ave., Cicero.

TYPIST
Bright beginner wanted who enjoys telephone work. Excellent spelling needed with typing 45 wpm. Mr. Douglas 555-5524

UPHOLSTERER
Fine opportunity for full time work. Seek individual experienced with fine furniture. Should know cutting. Apply Mon. thru Wed. 9-11am Personnel-130 E. WALTON
SHORELINE HOTEL

WAREHOUSE MANAGER
Northwest suburban glazing contractor is seeking an exp'd warehouse manager. Must be exp'd in architectural aluminum fabrication. Shipping, receiving and inventory control helpful. Send resume to:
P.O. Box 803883, M8443 Chicago, Il. 60680

Welding
Trailer mfgr. needs Layout person, welder, and laborer. I-55 & Rte. 83, 555-1505

TELEMARKETING
Need exp people. 3 shifts: 9-1, 1-5, 5:30-9:30. Work one or all shifts. $7/hr plus commission. Call Sue at 555-2684.

TELEMARKETING-Days or Eves + Wkends. Comm. or hourly jobs avail. Exp. pref. but will train. Tom 555-7788, 9-2 daily

TELEPHONE SOLICITORS
Reputable home imp. co. with 21 yr. reputation wants several full/part-time telephone solicitors. Expd only need apply. Sal., comm. Call 555-1641 9am-2pm Mon-Fri.

TENNIS PRO
Country Club seeking experienced tennis professional. Resume & personal interview required. (219) 555-0330 Tuesday-Friday, 2 pm-8 pm

TOOL & DIE MAKER
Must be experienced. 50 hour week. Top wages and all company benefits. Call S. Jones. 555-2600
Z-K Spring & Stamping
5050 W. Foster

TRUCK DRIVERS NEEDED IMMEDIATELY: Best pay and benefits program in the industry. Start at 23¢ per mile with regular increases to 27¢. Minimum of 2,100 miles per week guaranteed, no red tape. 23 years old with 1 year OTR experience. Good record required. Inexperienced? Ask about our approved driving schools. Financial assistance available. Call L.J. Owens 800-555-1533. For application and interview come to 7950 W. Joliet Rd., McCook, IL at 1 pm and 5 pm on Friday, Dec. 12th

TRUCKERS
If you are an owner/operator or want to become one we need you to run 2000 + miles per week pulling our trailer.
• Mileage pay empty/ loaded
• Teamster benefits
• Incentive bonus
Lease purchase available.
1-800-555-0867 US
1-800-555-2713 MI
EOE

Trucking
TRACTOR TRAILER DRIVERS
We offer a super opportunity for pros or students. Benefits include life, health, eyeglass and dental plus 18¢-27¢ per mile. Call our nationwide recruiter, 219-555-5982

Trucking
JOURNEYMAN MECHANIC
Must have min. 5 yrs. exp. on diesel tractors & be qualified to handle all phases of tractor repair. Call Larry Braxton betw 9am & 5pm 555-2995

B. Referring to the want ads, apply for two or three jobs using the following sentences as a guide.

1. My name is _____ . I'm calling about the ad for a

   _____ .

2. Do you have experience as a _____ ?

   Yes, I do. I have _____ of experience.

3. What does it pay?

   It pays _____ an _____ .

4. What are the requirements?

   You need to _____ .
      (e.g., type 40 words a minute.)

5. What is the address of the company?

   It's _____ .

6. What is the company's phone number?

   It's _____ .

7. What are the hours of the job?

   They're _____ to _____ , _____ through

   _____ .

8. Can you work nights?

   Yes, _____ . (or) No, _____ .

9. Are you available on weekends?

   Yes, _____ . (or) No, _____ .

10. Is it a part-time or a full-time job?

    It's a _____ job.

11. Do you want to apply for the job?

Yes, _____ . (or) No, _____ .

12. When can you come in for an interview?

On _____ at _____ o'clock.

C. In pairs, use these questions and answers to start a conversation about a job.

Activity 5

A. In pairs, practice this conversation at the state employment service.

Employment counselor:	May I help you?
Woman:	Yes. I'm looking for a job.
Employment counselor:	You need to register with us. Would you fill out this form, please?
Woman:	Sure.
Employment counselor:	How many years of school do you have?
Woman:	I graduated from high school.
Employment counselor:	Did you have any vocational training?
Woman:	No, I didn't. But I took typing in high school.
Employment counselor:	Do you have any job experience?
Woman:	Yes, I do. I worked as a waitress for three months. Two years ago I got my present job as a clerk-typist.
Employment counselor:	What kind of a job do you want?
Woman:	I'm not sure. I need to earn more money than I'm earning now.

Employment counselor: Do you like to work with numbers?

Woman: Yes, I do.

Employment counselor: The bank has a few openings for tellers. They have a training program for people with your experience.

Woman: Oh, that sounds good.

Employment counselor: O.K. I'll call them and make an appointment for you.

B. Answer the following questions.

1. Does the woman have a high school degree?
2. Can she type?
3. Does she have any job experience?
4. Why does she want a new job?
5. Where is the nearest office of the state employment service?
6. Did you ever register there?

Activity 6

Change the following sentences to the past tense. Then change them to the future tense. Practice them aloud first. Then write them in the blanks.

1. She earns more money than he does.

   _____

   _____

2. I have less experience than the other applicant does.

   _____

   _____

3. This job requires more training than that one does.

   _____

   _____

4. The steel company has better fringe benefits than the auto company does.

   _____

   _____

5. He brings home a bigger paycheck than his brother does.

   _____

   _____

6. She works longer hours than her coworkers do.

   _____

   _____

7. Des Moines has fewer job openings than Chicago does.

_____

_____

8. This ad gives more information than that one does.

_____

_____

9. Every year the manager gets a bigger raise than his employees do.

_____

_____

10. The man travels a greater distance to work than his wife does.

_____

_____

11. Women usually get better promotions than men do.

_____

_____

12. The first applicant has a better employment record than the second one does.

_____

_____

LESSON 16

Pursuing the Job

Activity 1

A. Taking the roles of the persons indicated, practice the conversation.

Ms. Rosaldo: Is this the Delta Insurance Company?

Secretary: Yes, it is. What can I do for you?

Ms. Rosaldo: I have an appointment with Mr. Anderson at 10:30.

Secretary: O.K. Please have a seat. He'll be with you in just a minute.

Mr. Anderson: Hello. You must be the person who called about the administrative assistant position.

Ms. Rosaldo: Yes, I am. My name is Emilia Rosaldo.

Mr. Anderson: Pleased to meet you. I'm Mr. Anderson. Come in and sit down.

Ms. Rosaldo: Thank you.

Mr. Anderson: How did you hear about this job?

Ms. Rosaldo: I saw an ad in the newspaper.

Mr. Anderson: I see from your application that you have experience as a secretary.

Ms. Rosaldo: Yes, I do. I worked as a secretary in Puerto Rico for four years.

Mr. Anderson: Why do you want this job?

Ms. Rosaldo: I want a job that has some responsibility. I like to type, but I want to do more than that.

Mr. Anderson: What is your salary range?

Ms. Rosaldo: I need to earn at least $300 a week.

Mr. Anderson: May we check your references?

Ms. Rosaldo: Yes, you may.

Mr. Anderson: Fine. I'll let you know by Friday.

Ms. Rosaldo: Good. Thank you.

B. Practice the conversation again, changing the situation so that Emilia

1. is applying for a job as an insurance agent
2. heard about the job from a friend
3. has no relevant experience
4. wants the job because she likes to work with people

Activity 2

Answer the following questions orally. Then write the answers in the appropriate place on the application form.

1. What is your address?
2. What is your Social Security number?
3. What is your middle initial?
4. What is your birthdate?
5. What is your marital status?
6. What is your height?
7. Are you a U.S. citizen?
8. Do you speak a language other than English?
9. Where did you attend school?
10. What is the highest grade that you completed?
11. What job are you applying for?
12. Who was your previous employer?
13. When did you work there?
14. Why did you leave?
15. Did you serve in the military?
16. Do you have any special training?
17. Are you under a physician's care?
18. Are you taking any medication?
19. Do you have any physical disabilities?
20. What are the names and addresses of two references?

APPLICATION FOR EMPLOYMENT

(PRE-EMPLOYMENT QUESTIONNAIRE) (AN EQUAL OPPORTUNITY EMPLOYER)

PERSONAL INFORMATION

DATE

NAME LAST FIRST MIDDLE SOCIAL SECURITY NUMBER

PRESENT ADDRESS STREET CITY STATE ZIP

PERMANENT ADDRESS STREET CITY STATE ZIP

PHONE NO. ARE YOU 18 YEARS OR OLDER Yes □ No □

LAST FIRST MIDDLE

SPECIAL QUESTIONS

DO NOT ANSWER **ANY** OF THE QUESTIONS IN THIS FRAMED AREA UNLESS THE EMPLOYER HAS **CHECKED** A **BOX PRECEDING** A QUESTION, THEREBY INDICATING THAT THE INFORMATION IS REQUIRED FOR A BONA FIDE OCCUPATIONAL QUALIFICATION, OR DICTATED BY NATIONAL SECURITY LAWS, OR IS NEEDED FOR OTHER LEGALLY PERMISSIBLE REASONS.

□ Height_______feet_______inches □ Are you prevented from lawfully becoming employed in the U.S.?__Yes__No

□ Weight_______lbs. □ Date of Birth*________________

□ What Foreign Languages do you speak fluently?__________Read________Write________

□ Have you been convicted of a felony or misdemeanor within the last 5 years?** Yes________No________Describe:

*The Age Discrimination in Employment Act of 1967 prohibits discrimination on the basis of age with respect to individuals who are at least 40 but less than 70 years of age.

**You will not be denied employment solely because of a conviction record, unless the offense is related to the job for which you have applied.

EMPLOYMENT DESIRED

POSITION DATE YOU CAN START SALARY DESIRED

ARE YOU EMPLOYED NOW? IF SO MAY WE INQUIRE OF YOUR PRESENT EMPLOYER?

EVER APPLIED TO THIS COMPANY BEFORE? WHERE? WHEN?

EDUCATION	NAME AND LOCATION OF SCHOOL	*NO. OF YEARS ATTENDED	*DID YOU GRADUATE?	SUBJECTS STUDIED
GRAMMAR SCHOOL				
HIGH SCHOOL				
COLLEGE				
TRADE, BUSINESS OR CORRESPONDENCE SCHOOL				

*The Age Discrimination in Employment Act of 1967 prohibits discrimination on the basis of age with respect to individuals who are at least 40 but less than 70 years of age.

GENERAL

SUBJECTS OF SPECIAL STUDY OR RESEARCH WORK

U.S. MILITARY OR NAVAL SERVICE RANK PRESENT MEMBERSHIP IN NATIONAL GUARD OR RESERVES

TOPS FORM 3285 (84-3) (CONTINUED ON OTHER SIDE) LITHO IN U.S.A.

FORMER EMPLOYERS [LIST BELOW LAST FOUR EMPLOYERS, STARTING WITH LAST ONE FIRST].

DATE MONTH AND YEAR	NAME AND ADDRESS OF EMPLOYER	SALARY	POSITION	REASON FOR LEAVING
FROM				
TO				
FROM				
TO				
FROM				
TO				
FROM				
TO				

REFERENCES: GIVE THE NAMES OF THREE PERSONS NOT RELATED TO YOU, WHOM YOU HAVE KNOWN AT LEAST ONE YEAR.

	NAME	ADDRESS	BUSINESS	YEARS ACQUAINTED
1				
2				
3				

PHYSICAL RECORD:

DO YOU HAVE ANY PHYSICAL LIMITATIONS THAT PRECLUDE YOU FROM PERFORMING ANY WORK FOR WHICH YOU ARE BEING CONSIDERED?   ☐ Yes   ☐ No

IF YES, WHAT CAN BE DONE TO ACCOMMODATE YOUR LIMITATION? _____

PLEASE DESCRIBE: _____

IN CASE OF EMERGENCY NOTIFY

NAME   ADDRESS   PHONE NO.

"I CERTIFY THAT THE FACTS CONTAINED IN THIS APPLICATION ARE TRUE AND COMPLETE TO THE BEST OF MY KNOWLEDGE AND UNDERSTAND THAT, IF EMPLOYED, FALSIFIED STATEMENTS ON THIS APPLICATION SHALL BE GROUNDS FOR DISMISSAL.

I AUTHORIZE INVESTIGATION OF ALL STATEMENTS CONTAINED HEREIN AND THE REFERENCES LISTED ABOVE TO GIVE YOU ANY AND ALL INFORMATION CONCERNING MY PREVIOUS EMPLOYMENT AND ANY PERTINENT INFORMATION THEY MAY HAVE, PERSONAL OR OTHERWISE, AND RELEASE ALL PARTIES FROM ALL LIABILITY FOR ANY DAMAGE THAT MAY RESULT FROM FURNISHING SAME TO YOU.

I UNDERSTAND AND AGREE THAT, IF HIRED, MY EMPLOYMENT IS FOR NO DEFINITE PERIOD AND MAY, REGARDLESS OF THE DATE OF PAYMENT OF MY WAGES AND SALARY, BE TERMINATED AT ANY TIME WITHOUT ANY PRIOR NOTICE."

DATE   SIGNATURE

DO NOT WRITE BELOW THIS LINE

INTERVIEWED BY   DATE

HIRED: ☐ Yes   ☐ No   POSITION   DEPT.

SALARY/WAGE   DATE REPORTING TO WORK

APPROVED: 1.   2.   3.

EMPLOYMENT MANAGER   DEPT. HEAD   GENERAL MANAGER

This form has been designed to strictly comply with State and Federal fair employment practice laws prohibiting employment discrimination. This Application for Employment Form is sold for general use throughout the United States. TOPS assumes no responsibility for the inclusion in said form of any questions which, when asked by the Employer of the Job Applicant, may violate State and/or Federal Law.

Activity 3

A. Taking the roles of the persons indicated, practice the conversation.

Mr. McDonald: I'm here to apply for the security guard job.

Secretary: O.K. You'll speak to Mr. Fernández. But you need to fill out this application first.

Mr. Fernández: Hello. I'm Mr. Fernández.

Mr. McDonald: Pleased to meet you. I'm Jerry McDonald.

Mr. Fernández: I looked over your application. You seem to have the qualifications that we need. Do you have any questions about the job?

Mr. McDonald: Yes. What are the hours?

Mr. Fernández: There are three shifts: eight to four, four to midnight, and midnight to eight. You change shifts once a week.

Mr. McDonald: What's the pay?

Mr. Fernández: It's five dollars an hour. There's no overtime. But we do have health insurance and one day of vacation a month. Are you interested in the job?

Mr. McDonald: Yes, I am.

B. Practice the conversation again, changing the situation so that Jerry

1. is applying for a job as a truck driver

2. does not have any questions about the job

3. wants to know why the company needs security guards

4. is applying for a job as a maintenance mechanic

Activity 4

Use either **that** or **who** to fill in the blanks in the following sentences.

1. I want a job _____ pays well.

2. He's the one _____ earns a big salary.

3. It's a company _____ offers good fringe benefits.

4. Mr. Yee is the person _____ sent me.

5. The opening is for an entry-level position

   _____ requires on-the-job training.

6. List two references _____ are not relatives.

7. You'll want to wear something _____ looks nice on you to the interview.

8. We need someone _____ has more experience.

9. It's a job _____ leads to a management position.

10. I have lots of experience _____ prepares me for this job.

11. She should make an appointment with the person

    _____ works in the personnel office.

12. You will enter a training program

    _____ lasts twenty weeks.

13. The company plans for employees

    _____ are 62 to retire.

14. It's the union _____ requires all new employees to become members.

Activity 5

A. Practice reading this information about fringe benefits.

FRINGE BENEFITS

Almost every job has fringe benefits. But some companies offer more benefits than others. You need to know the kinds of benefits that are available. You also should know the benefits that you want.

Sick days and vacation days are a fringe benefit. Many employers give one day a month of vacation time and sick leave to new employees. Often these days are cumulative. Some companies have a retirement plan. They take some money from each paycheck and save it for you. You receive it when you retire. Some companies also offer health and life insurance policies for their employees. Occasionally, companies give cash bonuses to their employees.

B. Answer the following questions:

1. Do you have fringe benefits on your job?
2. How many days of sick leave per month do you have?
3. How many days of vacation per year do you get?
4. Does your company have a retirement plan?

UNIT 9

Identifying Community Services

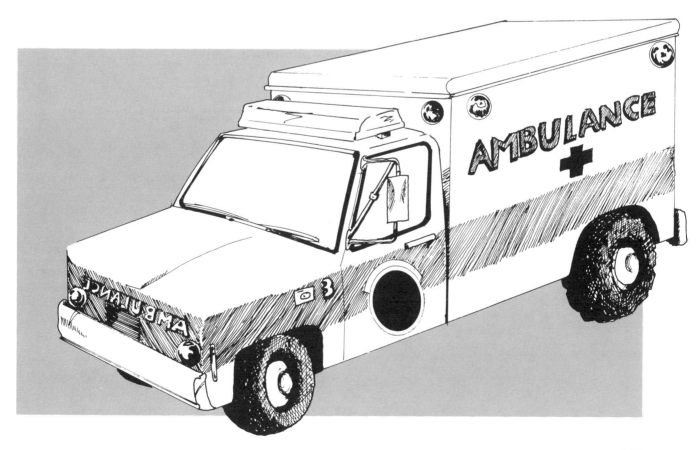

Emergency Services

Activity 1

A. In pairs, practice this conversation.

Wife: What a day!

Husband: Why? What happened?

Wife: Mike Kelly and I were talking at work. All of a sudden, Mike fell over.

Husband: What was the matter?

Wife: Apparently, he had cardiac arrest.

Husband: Really?

Wife: Yep. Luckily, José Treviño was standing nearby. He began resuscitation.

Husband: What did you do?

Wife: I called the ambulance.

Husband: How is Mike now?

Wife: He's in stable condition. The doctor thinks that he'll be O.K.

Husband: What are you doing?

Wife: I'm looking in the catalog for a course recommended by José.

Husband: What is it?

Wife: It's called CPR or cardiopulmonary resuscitation. It teaches you what to do in an emergency. I was scared today. I want to be ready next time.

B. Practice the conversation again, changing the situation so that

1. Mike fell and broke his arm
2. Mike choked on a piece of food
3. no one at work knew how to give mouth-to-mouth resuscitation
4. the company doctor was called immediately

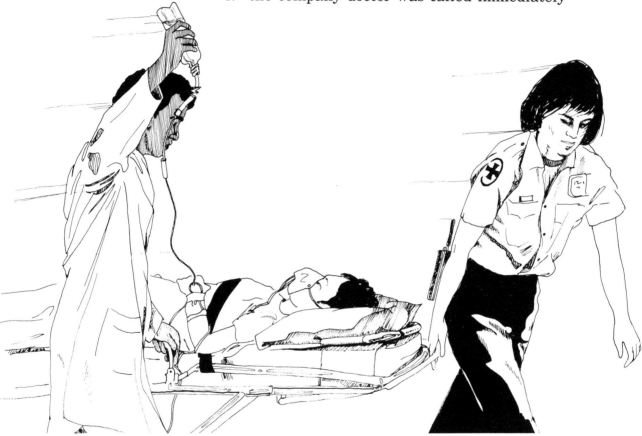

Activity 2

Change the underlined verbs to appropriate adjectives.

EXAMPLE:

They heard the <u>cry</u> child in the old building.

They heard the crying child in the old building.

1. The fire trucks stopped at the <u>burn</u> building.

2. The <u>steal</u> wallet was found on the seat of the subway train.

_____

3. The doctor put a tourniquet on the <u>bleed</u> leg.

_____

4. The <u>injure</u> man was taken to the hospital.

_____

5. The neighbors heard the <u>scream</u> child.

_____

6. The police say that <u>lock</u> doors discourage burglars.

_____

7. You shouldn't drive when you are <u>tire</u>.

_____

8. Smelling salts were given to the <u>faint</u> woman.

_____

9. The car accident was a <u>frighten</u> experience.

_____

10. The doctor had a <u>worry</u> look on his face when he saw the injury.

_____

Activity 3

A. In pairs, practice this conversation.

Victim: Did you hear the news?

Neighbor: No. What happened?

Victim: Our house was broken into last night.

Neighbor: Were you at home?

Victim: Yes, we were, but we didn't hear them. We were sleeping at the other end of the house.

Neighbor: How did they get in?

Victim: Well, the doors were locked and the windows were closed. We think that they came in through the garage.

Neighbor: What was taken?

Victim: The stereo is gone. The television is missing too.

Neighbor: Did you call the police?

Victim: Yes, we did. They came right away. Several other burglaries were reported in the neighborhood.

Neighbor: Gee, that's frightening! I don't like to live behind locked doors.

B. Answer the following questions.

1. Did anyone ever break into your house?
2. Was anything taken?
3. What did you do?
4. What can you do to prevent burglaries?

Activity 4

Use the following sentences as a question-and-answer drill. One student will look at the appropriate sentence and ask another, "What happened to _____ ?" (She or he will fill in the blank with the appropriate pronoun. The second student reads the sentence as an answer and then asks the next question.

EXAMPLE:

Sentence: I was hit in the eye.

First student says: What happened to <u>you</u>?

Second student says: I was hit in the eye. What happened to

_____?

1. I was helped by the paramedics.
2. The accident victim was carried on a stretcher.
3. Mr. Robinson was rushed to the hospital.
4. The drowning child was given mouth-to-mouth resuscitation.
5. The store was robbed by two men with guns.
6. The babysitter was frightened by the noise.
7. Her parents were awakened by the telephone.
8. Charlie was hurt at work.
9. The children were rescued by the fire department.
10. The broken arm was set by the doctor.

Activity 5

A. In pairs, practice this conversation.

Woman: What's all the excitement? Why are the fire trucks across the street?

Neighbor: The Olsen's house caught on fire.

Woman: Really? How did it start?

Neighbor: Someone threw a lit cigarette into a wastebasket in the garage.

Woman: Gee, that was careless! Who called the fire department?

Neighbor: I did. Smoke was coming out of the garage window.

Woman: Was anyone at home?

Neighbor: Judy was babysitting with the children. They were frightened but they weren't hurt.

Woman: That's lucky! Was there much damage?

Neighbor: Well, the garage was destroyed and the door to the kitchen was burned. But thanks to the fire department, the fire didn't spread to the rest of the house.

Woman: You're the one who called the fire department. You deserve the thanks!

B. Answer the following questions.

1. Did you ever have a fire in your home?
2. How did it start?
3. What are other ways that fires can start?
4. What are some ways to put out fires?

Activity 6

A. Practice reading these instructions.

Poisons or Overdoses

A **poison** is something not intended for internal use. An **overdose** is too much of a food or drug.

In case of poisoning or an overdose:
1. Find out what the patient took.
2. Call the poison control center immediately.
3. Follow their directions exactly.
4. Keep the patient warm.
5. Do not force liquids on an unconscious patient.
6. Keep a list of antidotes handy.

KEEP ALL POISONS AND MEDICINES OUT OF THE REACH OF CHILDREN!

B. Answer the following questions.

1. Where do you store your medicine at home?

2. Where do you keep your cleaning supplies?

3. Can children reach them?

4. What is a "childproof" bottle? Do you buy medicine that way?

LESSON 18

Legal Services

Activity 1

A. In pairs, practice this conversation.

Man: I had a frightening experience the other night.

Friend: Why? What happened?

Man: I was stopped by the police and taken to jail.

Friend: What did you do?

Man: Nothing! I was making a legal turn at a corner downtown. The policeman saw me and told me to stop.

Friend: What happened then?

Man: I was told to get out of the car. The policeman searched me. Then he took me to the station in his car. There I was locked up.

Friend: That's horrible! It's a violation of your rights. You have a right to know why you are stopped. You have a right to legal assistance. You have a right to remain silent, and you have a right to make one phone call. You have to insist on your rights in a situation like that.

Man: How?

Friend: Show the police that you know your rights and that you expect to have them.

B. Answer the following questions.

1. Have you ever had an experience like this?
2. What did you do?
3. What are your rights in this situation?
4. Was the policeman wrong?

131

Activity 2

Practice the following questions and answers in pairs.

1. Has the victim hired an attorney?   (Yes, . . .)

2. Have the boys' parents contacted a lawyer?   (Yes, . . .)

3. How long has she lived here?   (5 years)

4. Have you applied for citizenship?   (Yes, . . .)

5. Has he made a phone call?   (Yes, . . .)

6. Have you reported your change of address to the I.N.S.?   (Yes, . . .)

7. Has the person in the other car sued for damages?   (Yes, . . .)

8. Have you ever served on a jury?   (Yes, . . .)

9. Has your friend filed for divorce?   (Yes, . . .)

10. Has the manager filed for bankruptcy?   (No, . . .)

11. Have the members of the family been legal residents?   (Yes, . . .)

12. Have the suspects ever been in jail?   (No, . . . never . . .)

13. Has Mr. Peterson received a summons?   (Yes, . . .)

14. Have you ever had a problem with your visa?   (No, . . . never . . .)

15. Has anyone in the class taken the citizenship exam?   (Yes, . . .)

16. Have you ever talked to a lawyer?   (No, . . . never . . .)

Activity 3

A. Take the roles of a lawyer and a client. Practice the conversation.

Lawyer: What's the problem?

Client: Last week I bought a used car at the dealership on Sixth Street. The next day I was driving it on the expressway and the transmission went out.

Lawyer: Have you told the dealer about it?

Client: Yes, I have. I called him right away.

Lawyer: What did he say?

Client: He said that there was nothing wrong with the car when he sold it. He thinks that the repairs are my responsibility.

Lawyer: How much will the repairs cost?

Client: About two hundred dollars. What do you think?

Lawyer: You have a good case. I think that we should sue the used-car dealer.

B. Practice the conversation again, changing the situation so that

1. the clutch went out
2. the brakes didn't work
3. the dealer sold the customer a stolen car
4. the customer had four flat tires

Activity 4

A. Practice reading this newspaper article.

Boys Arrested in Theft

Two teenage boys were arrested on Friday night. They were charged with a burglary at the home of William Wilson on Bluff Drive. A stereo set, a color television a digital clock, and an AM/FM radio were missing. The theft was reported to police on Friday afternoon.

The boys are minors. Their names were not given to the reporters. This is their first offense. The boys will appear in juvenile court on Tuesday morning. The court has appointed a lawyer to represent them.

B. Answer the following questions.

1. Who was arrested?

2. What was taken in the burglary?

3. When was the theft reported?

4. Why were the boys' names not given to reporters?

5. Have the boys been in court before?

6. Who will represent the boys?

Activity 5

In pairs, practice this conversation.

Mai: What's new?

Van: We just moved to a new apartment. We like it a lot.

Mai: Great! But have you reported your new address to the Immigration Service?

Van: No, I haven't. Why?

Mai: Have you become a citizen?

Van: No, I haven't.

Mai: Do you have an alien registration receipt card?

Van: I don't know. I have a green card.

Mai: It's the same thing. Then you are required to report a change of address to the I.N.S.

Van: What do they ask?

Mai: They want to know your name, your alien registration number, your old address, and your new address.

Van: How do I report the change?

Mai: You get a form from the Immigration Service. They're in the phone book under the U.S. Department of Justice.

Van: O.K. I'll do it soon.

Activity 6

Answer the following questions.

1. Are you a citizen?

2. Do you have to report a change of address?

3. When do you have to report it?

4. What is the status of your visa?

UNIT 10

Securing Health Services

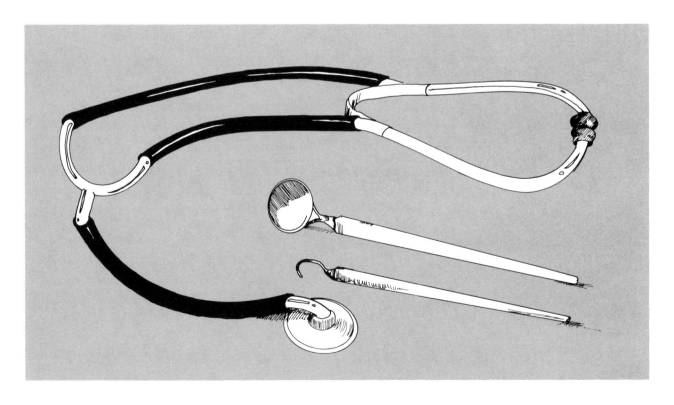

Preventive Health Care for the Community

Activity 1

A. Taking the roles specified, practice the conversation.

Patient: I'm here for my annual checkup.

Nurse: O.K. Come on in here. I'll take your temperature and your blood pressure. Take off your shoes and stand on the scale. I need your height and weight. O.K. Go into this room and take off your clothes. The doctor will see you in a few minutes.

Doctor: Have you been sick this year?

Patient: I had a cold last fall and I got the flu this winter. Otherwise, I've been fine.

Doctor: Have you had any other health problems?

Patient: No, I haven't. I've felt fine.

Doctor: Open your mouth and say "Ah." Let me look at your throat. Breathe normally and let me listen to your heart. O.K. Get dressed and go into my office. We'll talk there.

Doctor: Your temperature is normal and your blood pressure is fine. Generally, you're in good condition. But you should lose about ten pounds. You need to eat low-calorie foods and get more exercise.

Patient: I don't have time to exercise. I have an office job and I take the bus to work.

Doctor: That's no excuse. Exercise should be a daily habit. Could you walk to another bus stop that's several blocks from home?

Patient: I guess so. That wouldn't be too difficult.

B. Answer the following questions.

1. When was your last checkup?
2. Have you been sick this year?
3. What was your blood pressure?
4. Do you exercise regularly?
5. What kind of exercise do you do?
6. Could you build more exercise into your day?

Activity 2

Change the following sentences as shown in the example.

Example: The doctor always gives an X-ray **to you** when you have a broken bone.

The doctor always gives **you** an X-ray when you have a broken bone.

1. The dentist sends a notice **to me** when it's time for my checkup.

   _____

2. I want to pay a visit **to Ellen** while she's in the hospital.

   _____

3. Ginny won't be here today. She doesn't want to give her cold **to anyone**.

   _____

4. Has the doctor told her diagnosis **to the family** yet?

   _____

5. Show your rash **to the doctor**.

   _____

6. Let's take a book **to him** to read in the hospital.

   _____

7. The hospital will rent a wheelchair **to us**.

   _____

8. Be sure to buy children's aspirin **for Julie**.

   _____

9. Some drugstores will sell generic drugs **to you**. They are cheaper than brand names.

   _____

10. The nurse gave the shots that they need for school **to the children**.

   _____

11. The doctor will write a prescription for my allergy medicine **for me**.

   _____

12. I always try to cook his favorite foods **for my husband** when he's sick.

   _____

13. Read the instructions on the medicine bottle **to your grandfather**.

   _____

14. Don't be afraid to ask questions about your medical problems **of your doctor**.

   _____

Activity 3

A. In pairs, practice this conversation between a woman and her son's doctor.

Mrs. Cruz: Dr. Juarez? This is Mrs. Cruz. Roberto is sick. I kept him home from school today.

Dr. Juarez: What's the matter?

Mrs. Cruz: He said that he hadn't felt good all day yesterday. He was coughing last night. This morning he woke up with a headache and a sore throat.

Dr. Juarez: Did you take his temperature?

Mrs. Cruz: Yes, I did. He hadn't had a temperature last night, but this morning he had a temperature of 101 degrees.

Dr. Juarez: It sounds like he's getting a cold. You were wise to keep him at home.

Mrs. Cruz: What should I do for him?

Dr. Juarez: Give him two children's Tylenol every four hours. He should drink lots of fluids and get plenty of rest.

Mrs. Cruz: Should I give him cough syrup?

Dr. Juarez: Yes, that's a good idea. He should be better in a few days.

B. Answer the following questions.

1. Have you had a cold recently?
2. What did you do for it?
3. How long were you sick?
4. What was your temperature?

Activity 4

Draw a line from each description in column A to the name of the appropriate doctor in column B. Then fill in the blanks in the sentence with the words from the appropriate columns.

A doctor who ____A____ is called a(n) ____B____ .

A	B
sees children	surgeon
gives X-rays	chiropractor
treats women	orthodontist
works with mental health	gerontologist
takes care of teeth	radiologist
delivers babies	ophthalmologist
sees whole families	pediatrician
puts braces on teeth	veterinarian
fits glasses	podiatrist
treats skin diseases	gynecologist
treats bones and muscles	psychiatrist
does surgery	dentist
sees elderly patients	obstetrician
treats eye diseases	family practitioner
specializes on foot problems	optometrist
treats animals	dermatologist

Activity 5

A. Taking the roles indicated, practice this conversation at a dentist's office.

Patient: I haven't been to the dentist in a long time.

Dental hygienist: Well, I'm glad that you're here. You should see the dentist every six months. First I'm going to take some X-rays. Then I'll clean your teeth. After that, the dentist will look at your teeth.

Dentist: Have you ever had any fillings?

Patient: No, I haven't.

Dentist: Well, your X-rays show two small cavities. I'm going to fill them today. But first let's talk about daily dental care. How often do you brush your teeth?

Patient: Twice a day—in the morning and at night.

Dentist: Do you use dental floss?

Patient: No, I don't.

Dentist: O.K. You should brush your teeth and gums after every meal. Brush your teeth in the direction that they grow. Use dental floss at least once a day. Make sure that no food stays between your teeth.

Patient: O.K. I'll try it. I know that I should take better care of my teeth.

B. Answer the following questions.

1. When have you gone to the dentist?

2. Have you had any cavities?

3. Has your dentist recommended a particular brand of toothpaste?

4. How often should you brush your teeth?

Activity 6

Change the following sentences to questions as shown in the example.

EXAMPLE:

I had stayed home from work to rest.

Had you stayed home from work to rest?

1. The doctor had put the boy's leg in a cast.

   _____

2. The patient had been allergic to penicillin.

   _____

3. He had complained of chest pains before his heart attack.

   _____

4. As a family, they had exercised regularly.

   _____

5. The doctor had prescribed some medicine several months ago.

   _____

6. I had taken my son's temperature at bedtime.

   _____

7. The school nurse had kept health records on all of the children.

   _____

8. My daughter had had all of the childhood diseases before she started school.

   _____

9. After her fall, she had worn her arm in a sling.

   _____

10. My uncle had suffered from hay fever for his whole life.

   _____

11. The doctor had removed the stitches on Thursday.

   _____

12. The woman had never been pregnant.

   _____

13. He had sprained his ankle in a race.

   _____

14. We had called to make an appointment for our annual checkup.

   _____

LESSON 20

Health Resources in the Community

Activity 1

A. In pairs, practice this conversation.

Bob: Ernie, you've been living in this area for a long time. Maybe you can help me.

Ernie: Sure. What's the problem?

Bob: My wife and I have been looking for health services. We can't afford a private doctor, but we need to find a clinic or something. Right now, there's no place to go if we get sick.

Ernie: Well, you might try the Neighborhood Health Clinic. We've been going there for several years. We had been going to the clinic on Fifth Street, but my wife didn't like the obstetrician there. When she became pregnant with our second child, we decided to try the Neighborhood Clinic.

Bob: What services do they offer?

Ernie: They have a number of doctors. There is a pediatrician for the children. They also have a gynecologist on staff. They have a good prenatal program. Dental services are available at a low cost. If you need other treatment, they refer you to a specialist.

Bob: Have you been seeing a regular doctor there?

Ernie: No. We haven't always seen the same doctor twice, but all of the doctors are nice.

Bob: I have never liked to talk to a doctor in English. Do any of the doctors speak other languages?

Ernie: Yes, but if the doctor doesn't speak your language, the clinic has a translator.

Bob: Can anyone go to the clinic?

Ernie: Yes, but your fee depends on your income. They charge for services on a sliding scale.

145

B. Practice the conversation again, changing the situation so that:

1. Bob's wife is pregnant. They are looking for an obstetrician.
2. Bob's child is sick. He is looking for a pediatrician.
3. Bob has been looking for a different dentist.
4. Bob has been having chest pains. He hasn't seen a doctor in six years.

Activity 2

Change the following sentences as shown in the example below.

EXAMPLE:

I **have wanted** to change doctors.

I **have been wanting** to change doctors.

1. I **have seen** a therapist at the Community Mental Health Center.

   _____

2. Carlos **has not drunk** any alcohol for six months. He **has attended** meetings of Alcoholics Anonymous.

   _____

3. My daughter **has planned** to have the baby by natural childbirth.

   _____

4. You **have bought** your drugs at the pharmacy on the corner?

   _____

5. Planned Parenthood **has taught** couples about different methods of contraception.

   _____

6. The volunteers **have translated** for patients in the hospital emergency room.

   _____

7. Many senior citizens **have depended** on Medicare to pay their medical costs.

   _____

8. Our son and daughter-in-law **have wanted** to have another baby for a long time.

   _____

9. Attitudes about mental health **have changed** in the last few years.

   _____

10. Ann **has smoked** for ten years. She **has tried** to stop.

    _____

11. "Meals on Wheels" **has delivered** meals to older people.

    _____

12. The district health center **has given** T.B. tests and chest X-rays to community residents.

    _____

Activity 3

A. In pairs, practice this conversation.

Jeong: I have been so depressed lately. Ever since my divorce, I have been crying for no reason.

Hae: Have you ever talked with a counselor? Sometimes it helps to talk with someone.

Jeong: I couldn't do that! Aren't therapists for people who are really sick?

Hae: No, you don't have to feel that way. Attitudes about mental health have been changing. If you get help now, you won't have bigger problems later.

Jeong: Have you ever seen a counselor?

Hae: Yes. Last year I was seeing a counselor at the community mental health center. I had been having problems at work. They had been bothering me for a long time. But I wasn't doing anything about them. Finally, a friend told me about a therapist at the mental health center. I saw her regularly for ten weeks. After that, I felt much better.

Jeong: That sounds good. What services does the mental health center have?

Hae: It has a staff of trained counselors. They have experience with all kinds of problems. The center has been trying to hire therapists who speak different languages. One of their counselors speaks Cantonese and another one speaks Spanish. The center also has set up a crisis line.

Jeong: What's that?

Hae: It's a telephone that someone answers twenty-four hours a day. If you need to talk with someone, a counselor is always available.

Jeong: What about privacy? I don't want the whole world to know my problems!

Hae: Don't worry. Everything that you say is confidential. The staff is very careful about that.

B. Answer the following questions.

1. What is Jeong's problem?

2. Why do you think that Jeong is reluctant to see a counselor?

3. What services does the mental health center offer?

4. Is there a mental health center in your community?

5. Do other agencies offer counseling?

Activity 4

Change the following sentences as shown in the example. Pay special attention to the difference between these sentences and those in Activity 2 above.

EXAMPLE:

I **had expected** a check from the insurance company to pay for the laboratory work.

I **had been expecting** a check from the insurance company to pay for the laboratory work.

1. The family **had gone** to the Pilsen Health Clinic.
2. The drug abuse clinic **had treated** many addicts with methadone.
3. The public health department **had given** flu shots to prevent an epidemic.
4. The steel company **had provided** health insurance to its employees.
5. The adult education center **had offered** a class for expectant parents.
6. We **had visited** her at the hospital every day during her illness.
7. The Espinosas **had looked** for a doctor who speaks Spanish.
8. The family therapist **had treated** all of the members of the family.
9. Mrs. Yee **had worked** as a nurse's aide at the hospital.
10. I **had counted** calories to lose weight.
11. The dental students at the university **had cleaned** teeth for a low fee.
12. The suicide prevention center **had informed** the community about its crisis telephone number.

Activity 5

A. Practice reading this information about health insurance.

HEALTH INSURANCE

Medical treatment in the United States is very expensive. Doctors' fees are high. Hospitals charge a lot of money for their services. If you get sick suddenly, you will need medical care immediately. You may not have the money to pay for medical treatment when you need it. Health insurance solves this problem for many people.

Some companies offer health insurance to their employees as a fringe benefit. Often, companies have a group insurance policy. If your employer has a group policy, you will pay a low rate for your health insurance. Individual policies for health insurance also are available. If you do not receive health insurance from your employer, you will need an individual policy. Usually, individual policies are more expensive than group policies. You can buy an insurance policy that covers all of the members of your family. Tell your employer or your insurance agent that you want health insurance for your whole family.

Insurance policies offer different kinds of benefits. Many policies pay for your room and board in the hospital. They may also pay for X-rays, laboratory tests, drugs, and surgery. Most policies cover maternity fees for normal delivery, for Caesarean sections, and for miscarriages. Policies pay some medical costs for people who are not in the hospital. For example, health insurance may pay for treatment of broken bones and burns. They may also cover X-rays, laboratory fees, and diagnoses for people who are not hospital patients. A few policies offer coverage for dental services.

If you plan to buy health insurance, you will want to learn about the different kinds of benefits. It is important to choose a policy that will give you the coverage that you need.

B. Answer the following questions.

1. What problem does health insurance solve?
2. What is the advantage of a group insurance policy?
3. Why would you buy an individual policy?
4. What do insurance policies cover?

100 Want Ad Abbreviations

Below are 100 abbreviations commonly used in want ads. Next to each abbreviation you will find the word spelled out, a definition (if the word is hard), and an example or two of how the abbreviation is used.

Read through the list, spending a few minutes studying the abbreviations you don't know.

A

acct
1. account (keep track of money), as in "*acct* clerk"
2. account (business customer), as in "handle big *accts*"

acctg
accounting (keeping track of money). See "acct"

admin
1. administrative (managing), as in "*admin* assistant"
2. administration (management), as in "assist in *admin* of office"

adv
advtg
advertising, as in "sell *adv* space"

a.m.
morning, as in "call after 8:30 *a.m.*"

a/p
accounts payable (an accounting term), as in "*a/p* clerk"

appt
appointment, as in "call for *appt*"

apt
1. aptitude (ability), as in "*apt* for figures" or "mechanical *apt*"
2. apartment, as in "*apt* building"

a/r
accounts receivable (an accounting term), as in "*a/r* clerk"

arch
architecture or architectural (building design), as in "*arch* draftsman"

asst
assistant (helper), as in "payroll *asst*"

B

bkkp
bkkpr
bkpr
bookkeeper (keeps track of money), as in "*bkkpr* wanted"

bldg
building, as in "see *bldg* superintendent"

bus
business, as in "file *bus* reports"

C

clk
clerk, as in "shipping *clk*"

co
company, as in "*co* will train"

coll
college, as in "some *coll* preferred"

com
comm
1. commission (pay based on how much business you do), as in "salary plus *comm*"
2. commercial (dealing with the business world), as in "*comm* artist," or "must have studied *comm* courses"

corp
corporation, as in "large industrial *corp*"

D

dept
department, as in "sales *dept*"

dict
1. dictaphone (recording machine used for typing letters, speeches), as in "*dict* operator needed"
2. dictation (taking down speeches, letters, etc., in shorthand), as in "must take *dict*"

dir director, as in "*dir* of marketing"

div division (part of a company), as in "manufacturing *div*"

E

elect electric, as in "*elect* typewriter"

eqpt equipment, as in "heavy *eqpt* clerk"

etc and so forth, as in "insurance, hospitalization, *etc*"

eves evenings, as in "work *eves* and weekends"

exec executive (person with a high company position), as in "bank *exec*" or "*exec* secretary" (secretary to an executive)

exp experience, as in "no *exp* necessary"

ext telephone extension (each phone in a company has its own extension number), as in "ask for *ext* 272"

F

figs figures (arithmetic), as in "good at *figs*"

ftr future, as in "exciting *ftr*, high pay"

G

gd good, as in "*gd* opportunity"

gen
gen'l } general, as in "*gen* office work"

grad graduate, as in "recent *grad*"

H

hosp hospital, as in "*hosp* nurse"

hqtrs headquarters (main office), as in "ask at company *hqtrs*"

hr hour, as in "40 *hr* week"

hrly hourly, as in "good *hrly* rate"

h s high school, as in "*h s* graduate"

I

incl 1. include, as in "*incl* salary requirements"
2. including, as in "*incl* room and board"

ind industrial, as in "downtown *ind* firm"

J

jr junior (beginner or assistant), as in "*jr* secretary"

K-L

lt light (a little), as in "*lt* experience"

M

mach machine, as in "run office *mach*"

manuf 1. manufacturer (company that makes things, usually by machine), as in "city's largest *manuf*"
2. manufacturing, as in "*manuf* company"

mech 1. mechanic, as in "auto *mech*"
2. mechanical, as in "*mech* ability"

med medical, as in "*med* secretary"

mfg manufacturing, see "manuf"

mfgr manufacturer, see "manuf"

mgment
mgmt
mgt } management, as in "*mgmt* trainee"

mgr manager, as in "assistant to office *mgr*"

mktg marketing (finding new ways to sell things), as in "person to assist *mktg* director"

mo month, as in "earn over $400 per *mo*"

N

natl national, as in "large *natl* drug store chain"

nec necessary, as in "shorthand *nec*"

O

ofc office, as in "*ofc* boy or girl to run errands"

op
oper
opr } 1. operate, as in "must *oper* adding machine"
2. operator, as in "need multilith *opr*"

oppty opportunity, as in "good *oppty* for the right person

P

PBX telephone switchboard, as in "person to run *PBX*"

p.m. afternoon or evenings, as in "call after 4 *p.m.*"

pref
1. prefer, as in "*pref* experienced clerk"
2. preferred, as in "college *pref*"

pres president, as in "stenographer for company *pres*"

prod
1. product, as in "sell new *prod*"
2. production, as in "work in *prod* department"

Q-R

rec receiving (taking in), as in "*rec* and storage clerk"

recpt receptionist (person who greets people), as in "*recpt* for magazine company front office"

refs references, as in "give your *refs*"

req'd required, as in "selling experience *req'd*"

rm room, as in "apply at *rm* 1211"

S

sec
secy
1. secretary, as in "*sec* wanted"
2. secretarial, as in "must have *sec* skills"

sh shorthand, as in "must take *sh* at 90 words per minute"

sr
1. senior (experienced, high ranking), as in "*sr* secretary" or "*sr* clerk"
2. senior (last year in high school), as in "jobs for high school *sr*"

st
steno
1. stenographer (person who takes shorthand), as in "work as *steno* to company president"
2. stenography (shorthand skill), as in "must have light *steno*"
3. (*st* only) Street, as in "150 Main *St*"

stat statistical (work with numbers), as in "*stat* typist"

sup
1. supervise (be in charge of), as in "must *sup* four person department"
2. supervisor (boss), as in "call department *sup* for interview"

supp supply or supplies, as in "hospital *supp* salesman"

supt superintendent (manager), as in "building *supt* or industrial *supt*"

T

tech
1. technical, as in "deal with *tech* literature"
2. technician, as in "electrical *tech* needed"

tel
tele telephone, as in "*tel* order clerk"

tr
trn
trne trainee, as in "industrial *trne*"

typ
1. typing, as in "good *typ* speed"
2. typist, as in "*typ* wanted"

U-V

vp vice president, as in "work for sales *vp*"

W

wk
1. work, as in "factory *wk*"
2. week, as in "start at $70 per *wk*"

wpm words per minute, as in "must type at 65 *wpm*"

XYZ

yr year, as in "one *yr* experience as mechanic"